C000049132

Wellbeing and Quality of L...

Praise for this book

'For a better, more progressive approach to development we need better, more progressive indicators. This book provides a welcome and accessible set of ideas and advice on how to go about ensuring participation in developing new metrics for development.'

Duncan Green, Senior Strategic Adviser,
Oxfam GB

'This book clearly outlines key issues about community wellbeing and quality of life, linking them to concrete initiatives that open up many possibilities for practitioners both for consideration and adaptation. It will be an invaluable resource book for all those who want to deepen their understanding of the dynamic connections between community wellbeing, democratic participation, and community action.'

Diane Gillespie, Emeritus Professor, Interdisciplinary Arts and Sciences,
University of Washington Bothell

'Wellbeing and Quality of Life Assessment provides compelling practical guidance on how people-centred development can promote wellbeing and an analysis of why it should. Development practitioners, policy-makers, scholars, and others interested in international development in practice should read this.'

Ben Cislaghi, Director of Research, Monitoring and Evaluation,
Tostan International.

'The conceptual frameworks of wellbeing champion deep understanding and comprehensive analysis of why development agencies exist and do what they are doing. Yet to assess the quality of life impact of programmes, the authors bring us relevant cases and learning from peers, and imply that there is no quick and dirty way to know how we make a difference but "paying attention to the way in which people locally are thinking and talking about their lives". Go back to the basics!'

Mayling Chan, International Programme Director,
Oxfam Hong Kong

Wellbeing and Quality of Life Assessment
A Practical Guide

Sarah C. White with Asha Abeyasekera

PRACTICAL ACTION
Publishing

Practical Action Publishing Ltd
The Schumacher Centre
Bourton on Dunsmore, Rugby,
Warwickshire CV23 9QZ, UK
www.practicalactionpublishing.org

ISBN 978-1-85339-841-4 Hardback
ISBN 978-1-85339-842-1 Paperback
ISBN 978-1-78044-841-1 Library Ebook
ISBN 978-1-78044-842-8 Ebook

White, Sarah (2014) *Wellbeing and Quality of Life Assessment: A Practical Guide*, Rugby, UK: Practical Action Publishing.
<http://dx.doi.org/10.3362/9781780448411>.

Since 1974, Practical Action Publishing has published and disseminated books and information in support of international development work throughout the world. Practical Action Publishing is a trading name of Practical Action Publishing Ltd (Company Reg. No. 1159018), the wholly owned publishing company of Practical Action. Practical Action Publishing trades only in support of its parent charity objectives and any profits are covenanted back to Practical Action (Charity Reg. No. 247257, Group VAT Registration No. 880 9924 76).

Cover design by Mercer Design
Indexed by Liz Fawcett
Typeset by eGIANTS
Printed by CPI Antony Rowe

Contents

http://dx.doi.org/10.3362/9781780448411.000

List of tables

List of figures

About the editors

Sarah C. White is a sociologist of international development and wellbeing, working at the University of Bath. She has been researching wellbeing in developing countries since 2002, with a particular focus on South Asia. She directed the Wellbeing and Poverty Pathways project in India and Zambia (2010–14). She received her PhD from the University of Bath.

Asha Abeyasekera is a lecturer at the Faculty of Graduate Studies, University of Colombo, Sri Lanka. She has worked for more than 10 years as a practitioner and researcher in the development sector, focusing mainly on gender-related issues and psychosocial work. She was one of the lead researchers and Programme Manager of the Psychosocial Assessment of Development and Humanitarian Interventions (PADHI) project (2006–9). She received her PhD from the University of Bath.

Acknowledgements

This work is supported by the Economic and Social Research Council/ Department for International Development Joint Scheme for Research on International Development (Poverty Alleviation) grant number RES-167-25-0507 ES/H033769/1.

Foreword

Robert Chambers

Over the past two decades, wellbeing and quality of life have become part of the rhetoric of development. This has been a positive trend, for these words and concepts make space for and accommodate the many dimensions of the good life to which we aspire for ourselves and for others. This book brings together a range of pioneering initiatives to explore these concepts in practice. Comparing and analysing these initiatives shows that wellbeing and quality of life raise puzzles and challenges and present opportunities.

One challenge is the tension between universal 'objective' measures, such as those in human development reports, and the reality that what people seek and value as wellbeing is subjective and varies by person, gender, age, relationships, status, place, culture, and more. Also, subjective experiences of wellbeing are not static but continuously evolve.

Another challenge is that every language has its equivalent collection of words and expressions for wellbeing, all of which have different connotations and are dynamic and change over time. In English, as in this book, there is a plurality of expressions that are synonymous, to varying degrees: wellbeing (used on its own, or defined or qualified as inner, responsible, physical, psychosocial, or personal wellbeing), quality of life, happiness, good and happy life, human flourishing ...Given this pluralism, big question are then: Who defines wellbeing? And for whom? Do professionals define for other people, or are people convened and facilitated to define wellbeing for themselves? Pervasively, there are the questions to be asked in framing wellbeing: Whose language, whose meanings, whose categories, whose concepts, whose values, whose indicators (in these and other dimensions), and whose realities count? 'Ours' – those of 'us' who intervene, convene, and facilitate? Or 'theirs' – those of local participants?

This practical guide helps the reader to navigate these difficult waters and to recognize that the questions are important and the answers not easy. The nuanced reflections to be found here throw light on some of the difficulties and dilemmas. The challenge is to identify, test, and evolve processes and procedures to empower people to analyse and express for themselves their ideas of the good life, or good conditions of life, or the words and expressions they use for these. There is no one answer. But whatever their methodology, contributors stress one thing: that sensitive facilitation is vital to enable participants to reflect on their own, multifaceted meanings and to share these without distortion.

Until now, the initiatives to elicit personal, local, and cultural ideas of wellbeing have been scattered and largely isolated. This book takes us forward into a new space, not only by framing the debate within the current state of understanding, as it does in the first three chapters, but by bringing together different approaches and methods. As readers, we are then presented not with a fixed menu but with an *à la carte* selection of approaches and combinations of methods. Each methodology can be a source of ideas for inventive adaptation, like cooking a dish for a specific need and context. Any reader wishing to use a wellbeing and quality of life approach can adopt one of the methodologies presented here; or treat them as sources of ingredients, of ideas, of methods that can be adopted, mixed, and adapted; or used as the raw material or inspiration for innovation; or as the basis for improvisation or invention. This book can thus be taken as an invitation to creativity.

The opportunities opened up are significant. The utility and potential of a focus on wellbeing and the use of approaches like those presented here are many-sided. They provide means for escaping the reductionism of any one discipline, whether economics or any other. They enable many people to gain from reflecting on their values and ideals relating to the good life. Being enabled to reflect in such a way can itself be a positive intervention that leaves participants with insights, changed relationships, and ongoing processes: wellbeing analysis itself therefore enhances the wellbeing of those who participate. Outsiders who facilitate gain understandings that would otherwise be largely inaccessible, and that may better orient their activities. And the values local people express when describing their ideas of wellbeing can be credible and persuasive indicators for assessing the impact of interventions. They can combine in one measure or comparison how people feel subjectively, which has validity in terms of what really matters to them, and this adds to, qualifies, and complements conventional 'objective' indicators. Strikingly, according to these accounts, these approaches are win–win: participants find them of value, generating and reflecting change; and facilitators find them a source of significant interest and insight.

Let me congratulate the editors and contributors for their pioneering courage and diverse and inventive approaches. They deserve thanks for what the rest of us can learn from them: from their accounts of their experiences and their critical reflections on strengths and limitations. And let me hope that through the inspiration of this book, many more development initiatives will focus on wellbeing as a key dimension of good change, so that we can learn from local people what they want for themselves and their children, and give that priority.

Robert Chambers
17 June 2014

Introduction to wellbeing and quality of life: ideas, issues, and choices

CHAPTER 1

Introduction: why wellbeing?

Sarah C. White

This chapter provides a basic introduction to wellbeing in international development. It identifies wellbeing as a field of ideas and describes the main characteristics of these and how they fit within international development. It then discusses some of the different reasons that focusing on wellbeing is attractive to policy makers and practitioners, and some of the politics of the different approaches. It then provides a brief description of the main thinking behind some key terms: subjective wellbeing, psychological wellbeing, happiness, and quality of life.

Keywords: wellbeing, international development, policy and practice, quality of life

Introduction

Happiness, wellbeing, and quality of life seem to be all the rage. From the Government of Bhutan's commitment to measure Gross National Happiness, to the United Nations' 2011 Happiness Resolution, to the New Economics Foundation's Happy Planet Index, to Gallup World Poll rankings of countries by happiness, to the Organisation for Economic Co-operation and Development's (OECD's) Better Life Index, to the UK's Office for National Statistics' collection of data on subjective wellbeing, to indigenous movements in Latin America mobilizing around *buen vivir*, or 'living well', to government programmes, organizational missions, customer surveys, and staffing policies – everywhere, it seems, there is increasing convergence in identifying the promotion of wellbeing or happiness as the ultimate objective.

But what does this really mean? Have we suddenly woken up to a global consensus on what really matters in life? Are we all, at last, pulling in the same direction? Or are the same words being used to mean very different things? And if so, how can we get better at understanding who is really saying what? And how might we want to define and work towards improving wellbeing or quality of life for ourselves?

http://dx.doi.org/10.3362/9781780448411.001

This book is intended as a practical resource for people engaged in social or development policy or practice who are thinking about integrating wellbeing or quality of life in their work. It is written by a group of researchers and non-governmental organization (NGO) staff who gathered together to share their experiences of working on wellbeing or quality of life at the community level, mainly, but not exclusively, in the global South. We do not aim to give you all the answers – we do not have them ourselves. Instead, we hope to provide practitioners with a concise introduction to the field of wellbeing and quality of life, suggest some key questions to think about when working in this area, and present a number of different frameworks for readers to consider, adopt, or adapt in developing their own.

- Part One provides a brief introduction to key concepts and issues.
- Part Two presents a number of assessment tools that have been developed by NGOs and researchers and describes the experience of putting them to use.
- Part Three reflects on using wellbeing in policy and advocacy.
- Part Four draws together what has been learned and considers how this fits within policy and politics more broadly. The book closes with a list of further resources.

Wellbeing and quality of life: what do they mean?

Wellbeing and quality of life describe a field of associated ideas, rather than a single concept or definition. At their root, they concern what it means for life to be good. How people see this differs from person to person, including by geography, history, and culture, between men and women, by community, personality, and time of life. It is not possible, then, to give a universal definition of what wellbeing means. In fact, it is important *not* to do this, but to make space for people within a particular setting to define what wellbeing or a good quality of life means for them.

As a field, wellbeing and quality of life approaches share a number of common characteristics:

- **multi-dimensional:** going beyond the economic to a broader understanding of what makes life good;
- **positive:** an orientation towards people's strengths and resources, rather than vulnerabilities and what is lacking;
- **personal:** concerned with the impact on people's lives, rather than the narrow achievement of project or programme objectives;
- **focus on *quality* of life:** what people get out of it rather than what they have;
- **focus on *experience* and *enjoyment*:** people's subjective perceptions, not just objective achievements.

While people may define wellbeing in quite different ways, there is considerable agreement about the factors that contribute to it. These include:

material sufficiency; a dependable and attractive physical environment; good personal and social relationships; dignity and respect; meaningful activity; safety and security; mental and physical health; scope for agency; a positive sense of self; and spiritual nourishment.

Locating wellbeing and quality of life in international development

While the labelling is new, work on wellbeing and quality of life takes forward already well-established trends. The most obvious of these is the move to recognize poverty and development in multidimensional terms. It also builds on and advances the insights of livelihoods approaches, which see people's economic activity as a complex mix of priorities, strategies, influences, activities, and alliances that draw on a range of material and social resources. Like livelihoods approaches, a focus on wellbeing promotes an actor-oriented approach that emphasizes people's strengths rather than their needs. In common with Amartya Sen, wellbeing sees living standards as related not simply to what you have, but to what you can do and be – his 'capabilities and functionings'. From green politics and the sustainability movement comes the importance of considering environmental protection and promotion as being at the heart of wellbeing. The health sector locates health within a broader concern with quality of life; and intervention in situations of violent conflict and disasters has brought attention to the psychological and the psychosocial. Work on participation shows the importance of listening to local perspectives and ensuring that local people participate actively in shaping the change that is to come. This also draws attention to the fact that it matters not just *what* change is brought about, but also *how* it is done. Finally, feminist work on women's empowerment brings sensitivity to the impact of personal relationships, self-confidence, how people imagine themselves, and, more generally, the politics of the personal.

In practical terms, wellbeing or quality of life assessment may be used in conjunction with other tools or frameworks, such as participatory research or gender analysis.

Why work on wellbeing and quality of life?

There are a number of different reasons that explain why a focus on wellbeing is attractive to policy makers and practitioners. This section identifies some of the key issues, and introduces some of the politics in how they may be pursued.

From project-centred to people-centred

In project or programme monitoring and evaluation, wellbeing shifts the focus from the achievement of project objectives to the impact on people's lives. There may be informal evidence that projects have had a broader effect in terms of more generalized empowerment, for example, that may have a significant effect on the sustainability of the project. A wellbeing assessment offers an opportunity to track these effects in a systematic way. This is attractive not only in giving a fuller picture of what the programme or project has achieved, but also in putting people's own perspectives at the centre.

- Wellbeing assessment may be used to identify local understandings and priorities.
- Assessing wellbeing means broadening the scope to include aspects of life that the project is not working on directly. This can help identify unexpected consequences of the programme, both good and bad. It may also highlight important issues for further action, not considered in the project design.
- Subjective dimensions are included alongside – or perhaps instead of – objective dimensions. Objective here means dimensions that can be assessed by external observation, such as quality of housing or level of schooling achieved. Subjective refers to issues that only the people themselves can provide information about – how they are thinking or feeling about their lives.
- Relationships, among staff and between staff and clients, come into sharper focus. Do the ways in which people relate to each other foster wellbeing? This encourages reflexive practice.
- Ideally, assessment involves a participatory process, in which people are asked to determine what matters to them and what the indicators should be.

The practical issues that need to be addressed in making this shift are discussed in Chapters 2 and 3.

A positive and inclusive approach

A further attraction of working on wellbeing is its positive charge. This replaces the default negative orientation of many social and development programmes, which emphasize deficiency and what people lack, rather than their strengths or hopes.

- Wellbeing is an issue for everyone. It therefore helps to break down the divisions between those who deliver programmes and those who are the recipients of them. These divisions mean that programmes can often carry stigma and disrespect along with aid.
- An emphasis on hopes and possibilities can bring a new positive energy and unlock old prejudices and habits of thought. For example, a group from a run-down housing estate in London was asked to participate in mapping their area for inclusion on an internet site. The initial idea of highlighting dangers and deprivation fell on its face: people didn't want to add to the bad publicity already surrounding the place where they lived. But when the plan was changed to make it a celebration of the area and

the people who lived there, people joined in enthusiastically. Working together on the project helped them see their neighbourhood differently, and encouraged them to think about how they could improve it.

- Authenticity is a major issue here. It is easy for positive rhetoric simply to gloss over old patterns, leaving them unchallenged. It is also important that the negatives in people's lives are faced honestly and addressed.
- In addition, emphasizing people's strengths should not become a cover for denying them the support they need. For example, many people living in poverty in disaster-prone regions of Bangladesh are without doubt resilient and resourceful. However, this does not mean that they should be left to cope with their hazardous environments with no outside support.

Beyond GDP

The limitations of using national economic growth as the main development indicator have long been recognized. Wellbeing provides a more rounded, more comprehensive focus. There are, however, very different views as to where this leads. The strength of wellbeing at this level is its broad appeal. But this is also its weakness, leaving it open to capture by very different political agendas.

- Some see wellbeing as giving additional, complementary indicators (for example in health or education) with economic growth still in primary place.
- For others it raises questions of what is 'good growth': that the economy should be developed in ways that serve human fulfilment and are environmentally sustainable.
- Others use wellbeing to argue for a new economic model that promotes material sufficiency rather than growth, with alternative values such as social justice, environmental integrity, and human fulfilment at the centre.

A universal indicator?

Paradoxically, wellbeing may also be attractive to policy makers for quite the opposite reason: not breadth, but parsimony, or slimness. This is where 'happiness' comes in. If the ultimate aim of government policy is to enhance wellbeing, and if the best guide to people's wellbeing is how happy they are, then a single measure of happiness can seem a composite indicator of how successful government policy as a whole has been.

The idea of the purpose of public policy being to increase happiness (or 'utility') is not a new one: it goes back at least to the 18th and 19th centuries, and the Utilitarian philosophy of Jeremy Bentham and John Stuart Mill. What is new is the claim that, after long having to settle for income as a proxy for happiness, in 'subjective wellbeing', economists have at last a direct, quantifiable measure of pure utility. This is why the promise of direct measures of 'how people think about and experience their lives' (OECD, 2013: 3) causes such excitement in statistics offices across the globe.

To have a measure of pure utility would bring two great advantages. First, it would give a generic measure, not specific to any particular programme or project. This could then provide a common basis on which to judge the effectiveness of – and so choose between – very different kinds of intervention. Second, it could be seen as a global indicator, which could be used to assess the impact not of a single programme on its own, but of the entire range of government policy.

You will have noticed, however, that there were a lot of 'coulds' in the last paragraph. They were there for good reason. There are many grounds to doubt whether a single indicator of happiness – or even a combination of three or four questions – should be used in this way:

- It is difficult to know what such questions are really telling you. Is one person's 'fairly happy' the same as another's, perhaps in a completely different country context? Aside from such issues as personality or the mood of the moment, studies have shown that culture influences the way such questions are answered.
- The way people answer such questions depends heavily on issues including the order in which questions are asked, the number of options given as answers, and so on.
- Also, people may not say what they feel, but what seems 'the right thing' or what will make them look good, or – if they are being questioned in the context of an intervention – what seems most likely to secure further assistance. Of course, these issues arise with all kinds of questions, not just those concerning happiness.
- Happiness questions are very vulnerable to political manipulation, which makes them bad indicators for policy. People can be coached and questions can be framed in ways that will result in higher scores. People wishing to register a protest, on the other hand, can easily use such measures to do so.
- Even if you can get an accurate measure of how people are feeling, this is influenced by a wide range of factors other than the projects and programmes you have sponsored or implemented. Identifying people's happiness with the impact of your project or programme is therefore a major act of faith.

Wellbeing, happiness, or quality of life?

The paragraphs above show that wellbeing, happiness, and quality of life may be interpreted in many different ways. It is important to pay attention to the politics of how these terms are being used, as they can be made to serve very different interests. This is discussed further in Chapter 12. But what about the words 'wellbeing', 'happiness', or 'quality of life' themselves? Some commentators favour one term over another and others mix and match between them. Are there any rules about what the terms mean and how they differ?

The short answer is that there are no universally agreed definitions. There is a general consensus that happiness is essentially subjective, while wellbeing and quality of life may have both objective and subjective dimensions. Beyond this, which term is used primarily reflects a given disciplinary or institutional history. For example, in this volume some contributors talk of wellbeing, some of quality of life, but we all share a great many perspectives in common. The paragraphs that follow introduce some of the main approaches to wellbeing, happiness, and quality of life in the wider literature. Part Four provides suggestions of further resources.

The literature on wellbeing, happiness, and quality of life is large. It covers a range of disciplines from philosophy, through psychology, economics, health, and social statistics, to sociology and anthropology. Each discipline has its own areas of attention and inattention. For example, economics may have an extensive household survey with just a single question on happiness; psychology may do complex statistical analyses of subjective wellbeing scores, but pay scant attention to the social or economic characteristics of respondents. They all share, however, a yearning towards objective data, and an ambition to be policy relevant.

Wellbeing is often used in quite a general way, simply to indicate a broad-based concern with how people are doing. Figure 1.1 shows the main, more specialist approaches to wellbeing and quality of life, which include a subjective dimension of people's own perspectives on their lives.

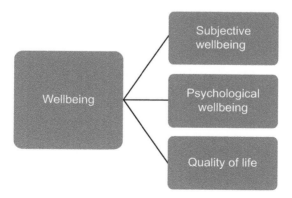

Figure 1.1 Wellbeing and quality of life approaches

Subjective wellbeing

The commonest approach is subjective wellbeing, or SWB. This is the approach that promises to deliver utility, and approximates to happiness in lay terms. However, it is a particular take on happiness: happiness as a measure to rate success in life. What makes you happy is not at issue, just 'how happy' you are. Advocates of subjective wellbeing claim that this slimness makes it democratic and culture-neutral: the methods can be used anywhere, and people are free to take pleasure in whatever they like.

In economics, the indicator may be a 'global happiness' question: 'Taking all things together, how would you say things are these days?' (Andrews and Withey, 1976). Within psychology, subjective wellbeing is generally seen as made up of people's satisfaction with life and the balance in their experience between positive and negative emotions. Sometimes these measures are used separately from one another and sometimes in combination. There are also many different ways of assessing each of these. While this might appear boring and academic, it can prove to be politically important: different kinds of measures give different kinds of results, and so different kinds of evidence for policy. Measures of satisfaction with life, for example, commonly correlate with people's economic status, while measures of emotion tend not to.

Psychological wellbeing

Psychological wellbeing is a fuller notion than subjective wellbeing, concerned with overall psychological functioning (or positive mental health). It is found mainly within the psychology and health literatures. Those who argue for psychological wellbeing are often critical of the subjective wellbeing view of happiness as being 'hedonic', or simply taken up with pleasure. They point out that what feels good may not be good for you, and draw inspiration from Aristotle in advancing a more 'eudaemonic' notion of a happy life being grounded in virtue, flourishing, and fulfilment, rather than pleasure. Critics of psychological wellbeing claim that it gives too much power to 'experts' to impose their own view of what makes for a good and happy life.

Quality of life

Quality of life approaches are most common in social and development policy. They may include some psychological variables or domains, but place these alongside other aspects of life, such as education, housing, income, and family and social relationships. They typically test for levels of satisfaction in relation to these. All of the examples in Part Two are quality of life approaches. Most of them combine subjective and objective dimensions.

The wellbeing cycle

Most of what has been said above assumes that wellbeing is a state that people experience. As we work with it further, however, it seems better imagined as a

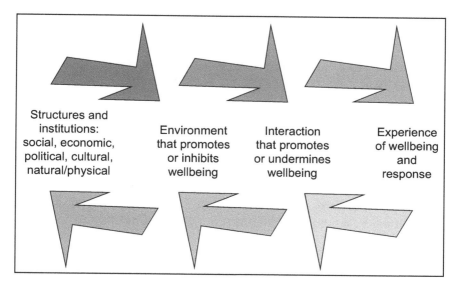

| Structures and institutions: social, economic, political, cultural, natural/physical | Environment that promotes or inhibits wellbeing | Interaction that promotes or undermines wellbeing | Experience of wellbeing and response |

Figure 1.2 The wellbeing cycle

cycle, which locates individual experience in a broader context of structures, policies, and relationships. Figure 1.2 sets this out.

Most assessments of wellbeing or quality of life take place at the end of the cycle, at the level of individual experience (far right in the diagram). Viewing the cycle as a whole, however, makes clear that this cannot be seen in isolation. The experience is the outcome of a broader cycle of cause and effect. Tracing the darker arrows back, this begins with the immediate behaviour of others around the individual; goes on to the environment that shapes this behaviour; and leads ultimately to the underlying structures and institutions from which this environment is derived. This is not to say that individuals' wellbeing is *determined* by this broader context – there is clearly a degree of autonomy, meaning that different people will respond differently to the same situation. The way in which the individual responds itself becomes part of the cycle. This is shown by the lighter arrows. The individual will act and interact with others in ways that promote or undermine wellbeing. This will in turn affect the wider environment, which will ultimately act to reproduce or re-shape the original structures.

Looking back and looking forward

This chapter began by discussing what wellbeing and quality of life mean, and the characteristics of wellbeing and quality of life assessments. It then located these in the broader context of international development thought. The section 'Why work on wellbeing and quality of life?' set out some of the main reasons why wellbeing and quality of life are attractive to practitioners and policy makers. This showed how the same words can be used in very different ways, with quite different political interests. 'Wellbeing, happiness, or quality of life?' described some of the main approaches within the field of wellbeing and quality of life. It emphasized the diversity of both concepts and measures, and the importance of paying attention to how these are used, as a way to evaluate the claims that are made about them. The final section presented the wellbeing cycle, arguing that *assessment* at the individual level should not mean that the influence of structures, policies, and relationships are ignored.

Having considered here how wellbeing assessment is advocated from international down to local level, the book now takes a narrower focus: the use of wellbeing or quality of life in guiding project or programme-level intervention. The next chapter considers some important general questions that arise in relation to wellbeing and quality of life assessment, leading into issues of practical implementation that are discussed in Chapter 3. Part Two follows with the case studies of particular approaches, and Part Three begins to scale up again with reflections on policy and advocacy. We return to the broader questions of politics and policy in the conclusion, Chapter 12.

Having introduced a range of approaches in this chapter, it is appropriate to end by stating where the contributors to this volume stand. Whether our immediate concern is natural resources and the environment, health, fair trade, or sustainable livelihoods, all contributors to this volume share the view that the key determinants of wellbeing or quality of life are ultimately political. Putting wellbeing at the centre of politics and policy making should mean a major reorientation of our current economic, social, and political systems. Wellbeing needs to be understood as emerging through social processes, rather than something contained within the individual. At the same time, we acknowledge that individuals do have some degree of choice in how they respond to the situations in which they find themselves, and this choice will have consequences for their own wellbeing and for that of others. While we differ as to the precise domains we identify, we all agree that wellbeing or quality of life is not reducible to a single 'happiness' indicator. Instead, wellbeing and quality of life must be assessed across several domains, with both objective and subjective dimensions. While most of the tools we present emphasize the subjective, this is therefore always in the context of other measures that monitor objective changes as well. Finally, and perhaps most critically, we share the view that a concern with wellbeing or quality of life must be accompanied by a commitment to economic and social justice and to environmental protection and promotion. It cannot stand alone.

References

Andrews, F.M. and Withey, S.B. (1976) *Social Indicators of Well-being: Americans' Perceptions of Life Quality*, New York: Plenum Press.

OECD, (2013) *OECD Guidelines on Measuring Subjective Well-being*, Paris: OECD Publishing.

Sarah C. White is a sociologist of international development and wellbeing, working at the University of Bath. She has been researching wellbeing in developing countries since 2002, with a particular focus on South Asia. She directed the Wellbeing and Poverty Pathways project in India and Zambia (2010–14). She received her PhD from the University of Bath.

Acknowledgements

This work is supported by the Economic and Social Research Council/ Department for International Development Joint Scheme for Research on International Development (Poverty Alleviation) grant number RES-167-25-0507 ES/H033769/1.

CHAPTER 2
Key issues in wellbeing and quality of life assessment

Sarah C. White

This chapter introduces some of the issues that arise in developing a wellbeing or quality of life assessment. It begins by discussing the relationship between individual and collective wellbeing. It then suggests the need to go beyond a simple divide between objective and subjective, and presents a model of five different layers of perspectives on wellbeing. This leads into a brief description of some options to guide the choice of a subjective approach. This is followed by discussion of some challenges in using subjective indicators to assess interventions.

Keywords: individual and collective wellbeing, subjective assessment of wellbeing, monitoring and evaluation

Introduction

This chapter introduces some of the issues that arise in developing a wellbeing or quality of life assessment. It begins by discussing the relationship between individual and collective wellbeing. It then suggests the need to go beyond a simple divide between objective and subjective, and presents a model of five different layers of perspectives on wellbeing. This leads into a brief description of some options to guide the choice of a subjective approach. This is followed by discussion of some challenges in using subjective indicators to assess interventions.

The individual and the collective

One of the common criticisms of a focus on wellbeing is the emphasis it puts on individuals. Some argue against this on cultural grounds – that, outside the West, people tend to think in terms of the collective, my family, and my community, rather than only about 'myself'. Others argue against it on political grounds – that responsibility for wellbeing can too easily be located

http://dx.doi.org/10.3362/9781780448411.002

with the individual. This can obscure the political basis of limitations people face and make the issue one of changing how you feel, rather than changing how things are.

There is no doubt that these are legitimate concerns. The best response, however, may be to sidestep the demand to come down on one side or the other, and recognize instead that individual and collective wellbeing must always be held in tension. Take the example of a housing estate with poor-quality high-rise buildings, little green space, and high levels of unemployment and crime. It is not difficult to see that this will affect everyone who lives there, making it hard to achieve the factors identified in Chapter 1 as contributing to wellbeing. These are the kinds of dynamics that the wellbeing cycle presented in Chapter 1 aims to express. At the same time, there will be some people living in such locations who nevertheless manage to enjoy a sense of personal wellbeing.

Similarly, feminist work on power within family households has shown that there are real internal differences that can have a material impact not just on women's wellbeing but also on the welfare of children and other family members. This does not deny the importance of the family's wellbeing as a collective – those same women and children may be highly invested in this. But it does suggest that *simply* looking at the collective will miss important dimensions of trade-offs and imbalances within it.

This is all fine in theory, but what does it mean in practice? If wellbeing is *experienced*, how can this really be assessed at other than an individual level? The only obvious answer to this is to have a shared process in which people from a particular family, locality, or organization come together to discuss and arrive at a consensus about their collective wellbeing. This carries the danger inherent in any such process that dominant voices will be heard and others suppressed, as is extensively discussed in the literature on participation. More specific to a focus on wellbeing, it may also mean that people will arrive together at a common agreement that does not reflect their personal realities. It may be, indeed, that we should expect this – that how people feel in a group will be different to how they feel on their own. A reflection on the comparison of collective and individual scores might therefore be built into the process of assessment. As will be discussed further in Chapter 3, it may be that the process of holding such a consultation will be as significant as the figures it produces.

The idea of 'responsible wellbeing' (Chambers, 1997) provides a different perspective on this tension between the individual and the collective. Targeted mainly on the relatively wealthy, this stresses that wellbeing becomes 'responsible' when it looks outward, to consider the impact that a way of life or form of experience has on distant others. Led by Roger Ricafort, International Programmes Director at the time, Oxfam Hong Kong took this idea and reworked it to argue that individual wellbeing includes social responsibility, involving solidarity with others and a duty of care for the world we live in.[1]

The subjective and the objective

As introduced in Chapter 1, wellbeing has both objective and subjective dimensions. These terms can be confusing because they are used in a number of different ways. In everyday talk, to say that something is objective is to say that it is true or unbiased. To say that something is subjective is to suggest that it may be untrue, or at best is just a personal opinion. In wellbeing assessment, we need to set these ideas to one side. Here, the objective is simply what can be assessed by observation – in principle, no one needs to be asked about it. It should be noted, however, that in practice much of what counts as objective is in fact reported by individuals, and the figures may be highly unreliable. This applies, for example, to much income and expenditure data that is accorded absolute faith in many surveys! In principle, at least, objective data stands on its own. It can easily be compared across contexts. The obvious example of this is income, with the $1 or $2 a day being used as international poverty markers. However, in practice even objective data may need to be set in context, because a dollar in one place may buy you much more than 10 dollars in another. Economists therefore adjust 'real' incomes by 'purchasing power parity' to try to account for this.

In wellbeing assessment, the subjective concerns how people are thinking and feeling, and this can be found out only by asking people themselves. Again, they may of course think one way and speak another, but ultimately the person himself or herself is the only authority – there is not even in principle a more reliable source of this information. Subjective data is essentially contextual. It comes from a person's (subject's) reflection on his or her situation in response to a specific form of questioning or prompt. The validity of extracting this data to compare it across contexts is therefore open to question.

In practical assessments of wellbeing, we have found that a simple contrast between subjective and objective does not work. This relates again to the tension noted above between the individual and the collective. It is also implied by the wellbeing cycle presented in Chapter 1, and its stress on the wider environment. Figure 2.1 presents a diagram of five layers, which interweave different dimensions of subjective and objective perspectives on wellbeing. This draws on the 'inner wellbeing' approach of the Wellbeing and Poverty Pathways research project described in Chapter 5.

An example may help to show how this works in practice. A wellbeing assessment concerned with health might begin by assessing how many hospitals, clinics, and health professionals are available in the area. This would be layer 1, the objective environment (the outer circle). It might also gather people's views of the quality of these people and services. This would be layer 2, the subjective environment. For particular individuals, the assessment might then ask what health services they have actually used. This would be layer 3, the objective personal. This could lead to questioning about what was good and bad about the services, and how satisfied the individuals were with them. This would be layer 4, the subjective personal. Finally, the

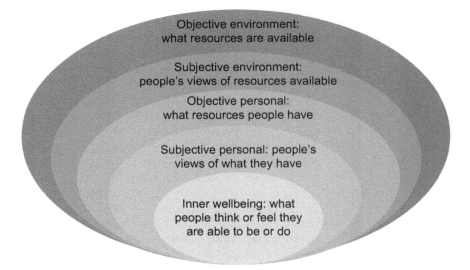

Figure 2.1 Layers of objective and subjective perspectives on wellbeing

assessment might seek to understand what their experience with the health services meant for the individual in himself or herself – did it leave him or her feeling anxious or frustrated, or confident or empowered? This would be layer 5, what we have called 'inner wellbeing'. We prefer this term to the alternatives of 'psychological' or 'subjective' wellbeing because it is broader and more open to differing cultural understandings of the relations between body, mind, and spirit.

Choosing a subjective approach

There is nothing new about using subjective data in project or programme evaluations. Layers 2 (subjective environment) and 4 (subjective personal) of Figure 2.1 have an established place in monitoring and evaluation. Information about these is typically gathered through group discussion or individual interview. There are, however, two ways in which a wellbeing assessment does depart from established practice. The first is the personal focus of inner or subjective wellbeing. In ordinary evaluations, the focus of attention is the project or service provided, even in questioning at layer 4. The focus of subjective wellbeing (how happy people are) or inner wellbeing (what people think and feel themselves able to be or do) is on the people themselves. This is a significant change. The second is the intention to put numbers on thoughts and feelings that are essentially qualitative in nature. The next section discusses some of the issues that arise from these two points. First, we set out a range of options as a guide to choosing a subjective approach.

The choice of which approach to use depends on your purpose in collecting the information, as well as the resources you have available. This is discussed further in Chapter 3. Here we set out four possible options. In practice, of course, you can also mix and match between them.

Happiness or subjective wellbeing. A narrow focus on happiness or subjective wellbeing has several advantages. It is widely used and straightforward to apply. The cheapest and easiest approach is simply to add in a single 'global happiness' question to whatever assessment you are already doing. Alternatively, or in addition, you could use one of the standard 'satisfaction with life' measures listed in Part Four.

The disadvantage of this approach is also its slimness. Is your 'very happy' or 'best possible life' the same as mine? What does knowing how people rank their happiness tell us? And how justified are we in interpreting such scores as showing the impact of our programmes?

Psychological wellbeing. This goes beyond asking how happy people feel, to finding out how well they are doing psychologically. A simple and widely used example is the 'Warwick–Edinburgh Mental Wellbeing Survey'. The shorter version has seven questions. The advantage is that you get a bit more information, such as whether people are feeling useful or connected, for example. A disadvantage is that it assumes a model of 'good functioning' that may not fit equally well everywhere. Also, it is ultimately a measure of emotional experience, which may be of use primarily in relation to a programme working on psychological or psychosocial issues.

Subjective quality of life (set). This involves asking people how satisfied they are with different aspects (or domains) of their lives. You could use a standard approach, such as the Personal Wellbeing Index (seven questions), which has been academically validated, or make up your own, to reflect those parts of people's lives where you expect your programme to have an effect.

The advantage is that this is still quite slim, but begins to give you information about different aspects of people's lives, which could be relevant for programme intervention. The disadvantage is that it is still very general, so may not tell you very much of practical use.

Subjective quality of life (participatory). In this case you ask people to list what is important to them. From this you derive a 'master list', either through a participatory process or through statistical analysis. You then ask people to rank how they feel they are doing on the different items. You can also ask people to rank how important they feel the items are to them, but this adds a level of complexity that may not be justified.

The advantage of this approach is that you have a list of items that people have stated are important to them. The disadvantage is that these lists can be rather random, including very different kinds of things, both objective and subjective (e.g. a nice house, well-behaved children, a good job, compassion for others). It is also considerably more resource intensive than the approaches described above.

Inner wellbeing. This is a fuller approach that involves asking people what they think and feel they can do or be with respect to specific aspects of their lives. Ideally, these questions are developed through a participatory process with the respondents themselves, working with a predefined set of domains.

The advantage is that it gives you potentially more relevant data that you can work on at a project level. The disadvantage is that, like the previous approach, it is quite resource intensive.

Whichever approach you take, your ability to put it to good practical use will be severely limited if you gather only numbers. To make sense of these, you also need to talk to people! More detail on this is provided below.

Using subjective data to assess interventions

Whichever approach you favour, there are a number of general issues that concern the use of subjective data in assessment. This section sets out some of these.

Attribution

Running across all of the approaches above is the issue of attribution. This is, of course, always an issue – how do you know that this positive change is really an outcome of this programme? – but there are particular difficulties when you are looking at such personal and subjective variables. In theory, it is not difficult to agree that self-confidence should be affected positively by a successful development project, and this might be interestingly explored through qualitative case studies. The effect of the programme on self-confidence, however, will be heavily mediated by individual personality and biography, by all that has happened to that individual in the intervening period, and by how he or she chooses to respond. This makes the path to self-confidence from any particular development intervention highly unpredictable, with either a detailed qualitative story or very large numbers needed to build a convincing case.

Getting personal

Clearly there are ethical issues that arise when asking people personal questions and in storing information that they have given you. Asking how people feel about things can trigger difficult emotions and it is important that an appropriate time and space is given to people to discuss these if they want to. In practice, however, we have found it quite common for people to welcome the new experience of being asked how they feel about things. Very rarely have they become upset by it.

A slightly different issue concerns the range of questions that should be asked. Chapter 1 mentioned a significant number of factors that are known to affect people's experience of wellbeing. These include their economic position, the physical environment, personal and social relationships, safety and security, meaningful activity, mental and physical health, and their sense of self and spirituality. Does this mean that a wellbeing assessment needs to consider all these aspects of life?

Practical issues that define the scope of a wellbeing assessment are discussed in Chapter 3. Here, the concern is more with the morality of different choices. Some people consider it unethical to ask about any aspect of life that is outside the programme's aims and objectives. On the one hand, they are concerned that this may raise unrealistic expectations. On the other, they feel it to be simply intrusive, none of the agency's business. The example usually raised here is close relationships. This may also be an area of life that local people are unused to discussing directly, making questioning particularly awkward. However, we know that close relationships can be affected by projects with a very different focus. Some credit programmes targeted at women who have few opportunities to use the loans themselves, for example, have led to a rise in domestic violence as the women have to badger their husbands for money when the repayment day falls due. This is an example where the unintended consequences would seem to be particularly important from a wellbeing perspective.

It is also worth remembering that what is sensitive differs according to cultural context – and that almost any evaluation asks potentially personal information about economic activity, profit, and loss.

Putting numbers on thoughts and feelings

In the West, we are so used to using numbers to rate our satisfaction with services or different aspects of our lives that we don't give it a second thought. In fact, however, answering a question on a one-to-five (Likert) scale involves quite a complex process of abstracting from and generalizing about our experience that is not at all 'natural'. Rating whether you agree or disagree with a statement is even more complex, since it involves understanding that the 'I' in the statement relates to yourself. Most people think much more easily in the concrete and particular ('give me an example') than in the abstract and general. Globally, there are also many people who do not read and write with ease. For all these reasons, getting answers to questions that can be translated into a Likert scale can be far from straightforward, and the more points on the scale, the harder this can be.

Even when you can get the numbers, however, a little reflection makes you realize it is a very odd thing to do. Why should you be able to put a number on your happiness? What possible meaning could this have?

The answer is that it has meaning only within a framework that values numbers rather than words. And the bias towards numbers over words has to be so great that it prefers numbers even in a case such as the understanding of happiness, where words are so obviously better suited. Unfortunately, when it comes to the assessment of programme or project effectiveness, we are usually operating within such a framework.

Numbers have two great advantages over words. The first and most obvious is that they allow us to quantify: to say *how much* difference has been made. The second is that they allow us to compare. They reduce the complexity of lived experience in all its colour, smell, and texture into a single figure that can then be compared with another figure drawn from somewhere entirely different.

At least, it can if you believe that the transformation of feeling into number also transforms subjective data into objective measures. If this seems a leap of faith too far, then you need to be extremely cautious about making comparisons between data drawn from different contexts, where the subject of that subjective data – i.e. the person whose views they represent – can no longer be kept in view.

A moving target: comparing across time

If it is tricky to compare subjective quantitative data across different contexts, this suggests that indicators need to be defined by the population concerned and then used with that same population over time. Even this is not problem-free, however.

- Wellbeing scholarship suggests that individuals' subjective wellbeing scores respond immediately when something especially good or bad happens, but tend to return to the original level (or 'set point') over time.
- It is well known that people scale down their expectations to adjust to disappointment and that their expectations rise as their circumstances improve – what economists call 'adaptive preferences'. One of the outcomes of a successful programme should in fact be to raise people's aspirations. The paradox is that this might mean they record a lower satisfaction score, because they now expect more at the end of a successful programme than at the beginning.
- The properties of the measurement scale also need to be considered. Any scale is fixed, and so limits quite severely the options you can take. If you answered five on a five-point scale last time but you feel even better now, how can you show this? This again shows that the numbers do not make any sense by themselves – *their meaning is intrinsically linked to the methods used to generate them.* If you are in any doubt about this, have a look at Norman Schwarz's (1999) paper 'How the questions shape the answers'.

All this has three major implications:

- First, quantitative subjective data cannot stand alone. It needs to be compared with complementary measures of objective factors.
- Second, you need to know what the goalposts are. What does it mean at the beginning of the programme to be living a good life? And what does it mean at the programme's end? The success of a programme may ultimately not be shown by improved scores but by the ways in which the goalposts that anchor those scores have moved.
- Third, quantitative data alone cannot provide meaning. For this, you need to talk to people, and record what they say through qualitative data. Otherwise, the meaning will be supplied by those who do the quantitative analysis – and will reflect their assumptions, values, and context, rather than those of the people whose perceptions were the source of the data.

Looking back and looking forward

This chapter began by arguing that there is not an either/or choice between focusing on individual and collective wellbeing – the two need to be held in tension. This was followed by a discussion of the difference between objective and subjective, leading into the layers diagram, which identified five potential dimensions of these. This also showed how different the current emphasis is on inner wellbeing or subjective wellbeing compared with what has gone before. The various options of subjective wellbeing, psychological wellbeing, subjective quality of life, and inner wellbeing were then compared. This led into a discussion of the difficulties associated with using subjective data to evaluate programmes. The main point here was to caution against lifting the numbers out of the context in which they were generated, and investing them with an independent existence all of their own. The meaning of the numbers needs to be understood in relation to the context in which they were generated and the method used to generate them. The further you get from this, the more questionable their usage becomes. Chapter 3 considers some more immediate questions that arise in developing a wellbeing assessment in practice.

Endnote

1. The other domains within Oxfam Hong Kong's 'responsible wellbeing' framework are self-sustenance, self-determination, and self-esteem.

References

Chambers, R. (1997) 'Responsible wellbeing: a personal agenda for development', *World Development* 25 (11): 1743–54.

Schwarz, N. (1999) 'Self-reports: how the questions shape the answers', *American Psychologist* 54 (2): 93–105.

Sarah C. White is a sociologist of international development and wellbeing, working at the University of Bath. She has been researching wellbeing in developing countries since 2002, with a particular focus on South Asia. She directed the Wellbeing and Poverty Pathways project in India and Zambia (2010–14). She received her PhD from the University of Bath.

Acknowledgements

This work is supported by the Economic and Social Research Council/ Department for International Development Joint Scheme for Research on International Development (Poverty Alleviation) grant number RES-167-25-0507 ES/H033769/1.

CHAPTER 3

Practical choices in designing a wellbeing and quality of life assessment

Sarah C. White

This chapter identifies some key questions that organizations need to ask as they consider undertaking a wellbeing or quality of life assessment. Process is important: how you do wellbeing assessment is (at least) as important as the results it produces. Investing in the process means extending discussion of what matters to people and communities, and improving the quality of the relationships through which development happens. This chapter shows that there are many different factors which will shape the form that a particular wellbeing assessment takes. Fundamental, however, is a central question: how do you balance the demand for quantitative indicators (outcome data, whether objective or subjective) against the claims of a more participatory process of learning as we go?

Keywords: wellbeing assessment, monitoring and evaluation, development intervention

Introduction

The aim of this chapter is to identify some of the key questions that organizations need to ask as they consider undertaking a wellbeing or quality of life assessment. Just as wellbeing is best thought of in terms of a process or cycle, so wellbeing assessment is also about process: how you do it is (at least) as important as the results it produces. Investing in the process means extending the discussion of what really matters to people and communities. It also means building up the skills of organizations, and perhaps communities, to strengthen the quality of the relationships through which development happens. In most cases, wellbeing assessment will not stand alone: it will augment, rather than replace, more conventional approaches to monitoring and evaluation. As this chapter shows, there are many different factors that will shape the form that a particular wellbeing assessment takes. Fundamental, however, is a central question: how do you balance the demand for quantitative

http://dx.doi.org/10.3362/9781780448411.003

indicators (outcome data, whether objective or subjective) against the claims of a more participatory process of learning as we go?

The impact on wellbeing or advancing wellbeing as a programme objective

The first question concerns how wellbeing is being used. There are two basic options. First, the enhancement of wellbeing may itself be the objective of a programme. In stating this, however, we need to recognize that this is possible in only a limited number of cases. While any intervention will have some implications for wellbeing, in practical terms it is unrealistic for a single organization, with limited expertise and resources, to take the enhancement of wellbeing as its programmatic objective. The breadth and multidimensional character of wellbeing means that it makes sense as an objective only within a closed institution (such as an elderly care home) or for a municipality or other local or regional government body that has a whole-population mandate and can mobilize a spectrum of groups and organizations to address a wide range of needs and interests. In this case, each group or organization might have responsibility for just one aspect of wellbeing. Readiness to work co-operatively with others would be an important signal of a commitment to the overall goal of enhancing wellbeing, but each organization would have its own more precisely defined objectives. The success in achieving wellbeing as a whole would be assessed by the municipality, for example through producing a multi-domain scorecard that draws on each of the individual project evaluations. In such a case, it is likely that the municipality would produce some generic questions that each individual project should answer, to make it easier to collate information across diverse projects.

The more common alternative is to focus on the wellbeing *impact* of a project that was not necessarily designed with wellbeing in mind, or where enhancing wellbeing is the ultimate aim or goal but not the specific objective of the project or programme. In this case, a project may be limited to a particular sector (e.g. livelihoods) or have quite a specific objective (e.g. the promotion of more sustainable farming practices). Initially, the interest may simply be to show the wider effects of a project, beyond the immediate achievement of its specific objectives – what does it mean to the quality of people's lives? Beyond this, however, there is likely to be some desire to move towards incorporating wellbeing in a more intentional way in project design. This might focus on *what* is being done, perhaps identifying an aspect of life outside the original project that is critical to achieving its ultimate objectives. Chapter 7 gives an example of this, as it describes how its Quality of Life tool highlighted for CAFOD the importance of looking beyond health to livelihoods in the organization's support for people living with HIV and AIDS. Alternatively – or additionally – the wellbeing assessment might draw attention to *how* the project is being delivered, and the need to ensure that relationships consistently foster a sense of recognition, dignity, and respect. Chapter 4 provides a particularly strong example of this, with the PADHI programme's 'core principles'. Within their overall 'social justice approach to wellbeing', these emphasize: the intrinsic value of each individual; sensitivity to the impact on social relationships; readiness to support people who experience conflict due to their role in seeking social transformation; and sensitivity to the power embedded in local cultural practice.

In most of this chapter we focus on wellbeing *impact* assessment, although many of the issues discussed are also of relevance to the identification of wellbeing as an overall goal. At the close of the chapter, Box 3.1 sets out some questions of particular relevance to the adoption of wellbeing as a programme goal. Some dimensions of the politics of this are also considered in the conclusion of the book, Chapter 12.

What do we want to achieve through the wellbeing assessment?

Chapter 1 suggested several reasons for undertaking a wellbeing assessment. The issue here is much more local. What is the particular motivation for this organization? What do we want the assessment to do for us? While this may seem obvious, it is not always straightforward as there may be a tangle of different interests, some very high-minded and others more pragmatic. However, it is very important to spend time on this stage, because it will have implications for the style of assessment you undertake and the kind of analysis you do.

- Is the main purpose to learn for internal purposes or to legitimate to funding agencies, to prove impact or to improve practice? If both, what is the balance between these?
- Is the main aim to produce a robust assessment of progress or to build capacity in developing a wellbeing approach in our work more broadly?
- Who will use the assessment: project participants, project or programme staff, senior managers, funding agencies?
- Who will undertake the assessment: project participants, project or programme staff, external evaluators?
- How will the wellbeing assessment fit with existing measures and practices in monitoring and evaluation?
- What does this mean for the kind of data we need to gather (numbers, comments, or stories; balance of objective and subjective) and the kind of analysis we need to do?

What does it mean for people at different levels in the organization?

It is not unusual for people at the top of organizations to be very excited by wellbeing, both as a new approach and as something that brings unity to the complexity of all that the organization does. By contrast, field-level workers may see it as a major new demand, without obvious practical relevance to their day-to-day responsibilities. Things are that much more complicated if the initiative comes from a (donor) organization with a funding relationship to the (partner) organization that will be required to implement the approach.

It would be ironic if the implementation of a wellbeing assessment undermined the wellbeing of those carrying it out. It is therefore very important to ask the following questions, with a real commitment that the practical concerns of those at the lower levels should be listened to in the ways in which the assessment is designed.

- How do people in different positions within the organization view wellbeing assessment?
- What are the costs to them?
- What might be the benefits to them?
- How can the assessment be set up so as to maximize benefits and minimize costs?

How will we define wellbeing?

This follows on from the previous point. For project-level staff to see the benefit, it may be particularly important that the assessment is clearly complementary to existing project objectives, rather than taking on too wide a remit. The question breaks down into three parts:

- First is the question of who decides. At one extreme, the chief executive may define (or adopt an existing definition of) wellbeing for the whole organization. As a middle path, an existing model like that of PADHI (Chapter 4), inner wellbeing (Chapter 5), or Wellbeing Wales (Chapter 11) might be used as a way to organize thoughts or generate discussion. At the other extreme, each group or even each individual may be encouraged to define wellbeing for themselves. The first will be high on consistency but potentially low on local relevance; the latter will be high on local sensitivity but low on consistency. Which of these qualities matters more and how to strike the balance between them will depend on how you answer the question above: what and who is the assessment for?
- Second there is process. Do you ask individuals what is important to them and distil common themes from their answers, or do you organize some kind of group-based 'deliberative process' in which people can debate and dispute and – hopefully – come to a common view? The organization of groups clearly needs to follow learning from participatory methods on how to enable people in socially subordinate positions to speak, but there are still questions about whether people in a group will state their 'true' feelings. Alternatively, the animated collective reflection generated in a group might be seen as itself part of the process of moving towards a wellbeing approach.
- Third there is the content. As stated in Chapter 1, material sufficiency, a dependable and attractive physical environment, good personal and

social relationships, meaningful activity, dignity and respect, safety and security, mental and physical health, scope for agency, a positive sense of self, and spiritual nourishment have all been shown to be important factors in promoting the experience of wellbeing. That is a lot for any assessment to try to cover! On the other hand, if you exclude some dimensions as not being relevant to your programme, you are limiting the potential spill-over effects, or areas of complementary need, that you can take into account.

Comprehensive confusion!

In most cases, a broad-based understanding of wellbeing will need to be distilled into a narrower model that can be assessed in practice. When it is too loosely defined, wellbeing can comprise everything – or nothing. This leads to two practical dangers:

- The multifaceted character of wellbeing could mean that all projects are expected to do everything. In particular, this may mean that a lot of 'social' activities are added on to 'technical' projects, even where this places considerable strain on the partners' capacity and expertise.
- Wellbeing language and indicators may be added randomly into programmes where they don't really belong, just to please the funders. At a minimum, this could lead to a 're-translation' (existing targets being reclassified as dimensions of wellbeing); at worst, it could add confusion and an extra burden into monitoring and evaluation systems.

One way to guard against this is to ask about the added value of working on wellbeing:

- Does a new focus on wellbeing add anything to what you are already doing? Does it mean you can take something away from what you are already doing?

Another way to put this is to ask the following question:

- If the project met its objectives, yet did not enhance wellbeing, how would you know, and would you consider the project to have failed?

If it is to be useful, wellbeing needs to offer more than just a new description for old values. In particular, it needs to be independently testable. This means that a project might succeed in its primary objective (increase local employment) *and yet fail to enhance wellbeing*. For example, a horticulture project producing flowers for export might increase employment in a rural area of Ethiopia, but it could be paying low wages and exposing workers to harmful chemicals. School-aged children may also be drawn to work there and as a consequence neglect or give up their studies, resulting in longer-term harm to their prospects. People may also have been dispossessed from their homes and farms in order to make land available for the new enterprise. This may seem an extreme example, but such things are actually very common. One of the primary values of taking a wellbeing approach may be its potential to question the human and environmental impact of what goes by the name of development.[1]

What resources do we have to commit to the assessment?

As with many of the questions in this chapter, the issue of resources is common to all monitoring and evaluation. It includes people, time, and financial resources. It also includes all stages of gathering, analysing, and using the information. An assessment of these factors may require you to revisit some of the decisions you made in the paragraphs above. Realism may require you to define wellbeing in a more uniform and less comprehensive way than you would choose to in an ideal world.

A subsidiary part of this is the question of who is best suited to undertake the assessment – project participants themselves, existing staff, or outsiders?

- Participants are obviously the people who know best about their own wellbeing. However, they may need a lot of support in translating this everyday knowledge into the more abstract categories of domains or indicators for assessment. As always, a balance will need to be struck between enabling participation on the one hand and adding inappropriate burdens on time and other resources on the other.
- Programme staff will know the work best but will also have a strong interest in particular outcomes of the assessment. The nature of their relationships with participants will have a strong effect on the accuracy of the information gathered. In particular, participants may find it difficult to be honest with them if there are problems with the programme. Many staff are already fully committed, with little time to undertake additional responsibilities.
- Outsider evaluators should be more 'objective', but it may take time for participants to trust them. Much of the learning generated through the assessment may be lost when the evaluator leaves, so capacity building will be much more limited unless a training element is also built in.
- As wellbeing assessment is quite new, there is also limited expertise available. This may relate to:
    - conceptual understandings of wellbeing and different approaches to it;
    - skills in distilling a workable model from the breadth of possible dimensions;
    - skills in identifying appropriate indicators;
    - skills in facilitating participatory discussions;
    - skills in eliciting precise quantitative responses;

    –   skills in recording, especially qualitative data;
    –   skills in analysing quantitative and qualitative data;
    –   skills in reporting on quantitative and qualitative data analysis.

- Does it make better sense to invest in wellbeing training for your own staff or for external consultants?
- Finally, at a very practical level, are there translation issues to consider, and have sufficient time and resources been allocated to ensure that this is done well? Translation, of course, is an issue in much monitoring and evaluation work. For wellbeing assessment there are particular concerns relating to the sensitivity and personal nature of some dimensions. These can require especially strong listening skills, and may mean that guidelines for facilitation need to be carefully translated, in addition to the questions themselves.

Wellbeing as programme objective

As mentioned above, in some cases the enhancement of wellbeing may be identified as the overall objective of a funding or programme portfolio. This is particularly likely where a number of organizations come together, perhaps at the invitation of the local government authority, to consider the interests of an area as a whole. This has the value of ensuring a broad-based response to different issues, populations, and needs, while not diverting individual projects from their particular purposes, or risking the 'comprehensive confusion' noted above.

Box 3.1 briefly outlines the questions that would need to be asked when adopting enhanced wellbeing as a programme objective. In broad terms, these concern *what* is done, and/or *with whom* it is done, and/or *how* it is done. The answers will differ significantly according to who is asked, and how respondents are located in power structures locally or within the development process. This recognition needs to be built into any process for exploring these questions.

Looking back and looking forward

This chapter has identified some of the questions agencies need to consider when developing a wellbeing assessment. While these may seem daunting, many are common to any kind of project evaluation, and careful preparation at the design stage will be repaid by the quality of the assessment further down the line. This chapter brings Part One of the book to a close. Part Two presents how particular research projects and development agencies have applied wellbeing and quality of life assessment in practice.

Box 3.1 Adopting wellbeing as the overall programme objective

- The *what*: Does our programme profile promote wellbeing?
  This question directs attention to the type of projects and programmes in the portfolio.

  - Are there some projects or programmes that promote and/or attend to each of the different domains of wellbeing we have identified?
    - ○ Is the area as a whole strong on one of these and weak on another? Is there scope for some rebalancing, through taking on new projects and/or dropping or redirecting existing ones?

  - Are there some projects or programmes that target more than one of these aspects?
    - ○ Is appropriate monitoring in place to track the relationships between them?

  - Are there processes in place to co-ordinate activities across projects?
    - ○ If so, are specific monitoring and learning resources being allocated to these?

  - Are there clear activities and indicators that demonstrate how objectives will be achieved?

- The *who*: Are our staff and partners well equipped to promote wellbeing?
  This question directs attention to the capacity of the umbrella agency and its partners.

  - Do staff understand wellbeing and the different dimensions of it that we have identified?
    - ○ Are staff strong in one of the areas and weak in others? Is there scope for some rebalancing, through making new appointments and/or giving additional training to existing staff?

  - Are we working with the right partners? Are some strong in their understanding and capacity to promote each of the domains of wellbeing that we have identified?
    - ○ Is the programme as a whole strong on one of these domains and weak on others? Is there scope for some rebalancing, through taking on new partners and/ or dropping or giving training to existing ones?
    - ○ Is the agency facilitating sharing and learning between partners, particularly across different areas of strength?

  - Are there clear activities and indicators that demonstrate how these objectives will be achieved?

- The *how*: Does the way we work with our staff, partners, and communities help promote wellbeing?
  This question directs attention to the way in which relationships are conducted.

  - Do staff thinking and practice when interacting among themselves and with partners promote people's dignity, enhance their scope for agency, and so on?
    - ○ How do institutional structures, culture, or processes affect this?
    - ○ How are staff supported in reflecting on and improving their practice?

  - Do partners' thinking and practice when interacting within their organizations and with local communities reflect these principles of wellbeing?
    - ○ How do institutional structures, culture, or processes affect this?
    - ○ How are partners supported in reflecting on and improving their practice?

  - Are there clear activities and indicators to monitor these elements?

Endnote

1. For an example of this in the Wellbeing Pathways research (Chapter 5), see 'The Politics of Wellbeing, Conservation and Development in Chiawa, Zambia'. Available at <www.wellbeingpathways.org/resources/briefing-papers/176-briefing-paper2> [accessed 16 June 2014].

Sarah C. White is a sociologist of international development and wellbeing, working at the University of Bath. She has been researching wellbeing in developing countries since 2002, with a particular focus on South Asia. She directed the Wellbeing and Poverty Pathways project in India and Zambia (2010–14). She received her PhD from the University of Bath.

Acknowledgements

This work is supported by the Economic and Social Research Council/Department for International Development Joint Scheme for Research on International Development (Poverty Alleviation) grant number RES-167-25-0507 ES/H033769/1.

Wellbeing and quality of life in development practice

Part Two of this book presents a variety of frameworks and tools that have been developed by non-governmental organizations (NGOs) and researchers, with a long history of working with communities in the field of international development, to assess wellbeing and the quality of life of individuals, families, and communities in the global South. Their interest in people's wellbeing has mainly stemmed from adopting a more integrated and holistic approach to service provision with the specific objective of improving people's overall quality of life. In making this shift, these organizations and institutions have also felt the need to come up with a framework with which to understand what wellbeing means to people, as well as to devise simple tools to assess the impact of development projects and programmes on a person's wellbeing, or to measure how effective a programme has been in improving a person's quality of life.

Each of the chapters in this section follows a similar format. The introduction explains the context in which the wellbeing framework or assessment tool was developed. The chapter goes on to describe the framework or tool including its aims, key concepts, and principles, and then explains how to use it. This is followed by a broader discussion of the aims and objectives of the framework or tool: what kinds of information does it capture? For what purposes can the information be used? And in what contexts can the framework be used? A case study is then presented to illustrate how the framework has been applied in practice. The chapter ends by reflecting on the strengths and limitations of the framework or tool.

Chapters 4 and 5 present frameworks on wellbeing that provide a conceptual map with which to understand the multidimensional nature of wellbeing. PADHI's psychosocial framework discussed in **Chapter 4** attempts to capture both the psychological and social dimensions that contribute to people's sense of wellbeing. Developed by the University of Colombo (Sri Lanka) following empirical research in conflict-affected and tsunami-affected communities, the PADHI framework advocates for a social justice approach to promoting wellbeing by including in its framework a discussion on how power and identity mediate people's wellbeing, as well as the importance of systems and institutions in enabling wellbeing. **Chapter 5** introduces the concept of 'inner wellbeing' (IWB) – an approach to wellbeing assessment developed by the Wellbeing and Poverty Pathways project (WPP) at the University of Bath. It offers: a model that encompasses the material, relational, and personal dimensions of a person's wellbeing; a new perspective on understanding the subjective dimensions of wellbeing; and a methodology that uses standard objective economic indicators as well as people's subjective perceptions and reflections to assess wellbeing in quantitative terms. The PADHI and IWB frameworks can be used at both ends of a programme cycle: to design an effective intervention by mapping people's needs and issues into the different domains; and to work out on what aspects of a person's wellbeing a programme is having an impact.

Chapters 6, 7, and 8 present easy-to-use assessment tools with which to measure wellbeing and quality of life. In **Chapter 6**, Traidcraft discusses how it adapted the IWB approach to assess 'human flourishing' – a concept that looks beyond the material dimensions of a person's quality of life. A group-based survey was developed and piloted in Bangladesh to understand the impact of Traidcraft's programmes on individual and community flourishing. Drawing from this experience, the chapter includes valuable insights and advice to practitioners considering undertaking wellbeing assessment. In **Chapter 7**, CAFOD presents its Batteries Tool – a simple yet effective participatory tool for people living with and affected by HIV to assess changes in their quality of life. The chapter describes how the information gathered from the tool is used by different stakeholders: individuals and communities have found it empowering because it helps them reflect on what they can do to improve the quality of their life; and CAFOD's programme staff have found it effective in improving case management, as well as useful for monitoring the overall impact of their programmes on people's quality of life. Trócaire's 'Wheel' tool, presented in **Chapter 8**, has also been effective in assessing the impact of its HIV programmes on people's quality of life. The Wheel is a participatory tool and has been effectively used to facilitate discussions between project workers and programme partners. The chapter provides detailed case studies that demonstrate how the information gathered from the tool can be used for monitoring at the individual and programme level.

While the authors of these three chapters acknowledge the limitations of these tools, a strength the tools all share is the potential for measuring wellbeing or quality of life over time, which can help organizations assess the impact their interventions are having on people's lives.

CHAPTER 4

A social justice approach to wellbeing: the PADHI psychosocial framework[1]

Asha Abeyasekera

This chapter introduces a psychosocial framework for understanding wellbeing and for assessing the impact of development and humanitarian interventions. It begins by setting the context in which the need for a framework to both understand wellbeing and assess the impact of development and humanitarian interventions was felt in Sri Lanka, and the rationale for incorporating local understandings of wellbeing as well as concepts such as 'suffering' and 'distress' into the framework. The chapter provides a comprehensive description of the framework, which has three key dimensions: how wellbeing is constituted; what mediates wellbeing; and the enabling environment required for experiencing wellbeing. It then sets out the core principles of the framework and explains why adopting a social justice approach to wellbeing is critical when addressing injustice and social exclusion. The chapter ends with an example of how to use the framework in development planning.

Keywords: psychosocial, wellbeing, wellbeing assessment, development intervention, development planning, social justice, power, Sri Lanka

Introduction

The Psychosocial Assessment of Development and Humanitarian Interventions (PADHI) programme was established in 2006 at the Social Policy Analysis and Research Centre (SPARC) of the Faculty of Arts, University of Colombo, Sri Lanka. The research programme was established as a response to the unprecedented expansion of 'psychosocial' interventions, firstly within the humanitarian sector and subsequently in development programming, in the aftermath of the December 2004 tsunami.

There has been an ongoing critique of the development and humanitarian sectors in Sri Lanka for being culturally insensitive. Disregarding caste and class dynamics in communities, for example, has sometimes led to powerful

http://dx.doi.org/10.3362/9781780448411.004

groups withholding their support for projects or less powerful groups being excluded from interventions – which has often aggravated divisions and conflicts in communities. In framing both problems and solutions using generic frameworks often developed in the 'West', the sectors have faced criticism for not responding adequately and appropriately to the needs of the local communities with whom they are working. This dissatisfaction became acute following the influx of international non-governmental organizations (NGOs) in the aftermath of the tsunami in December 2004. Many of the new entrants were criticized for hastily putting together programmes without first understanding the cultural and socio-political context in which they were working. Such interventions included a clown who walked the streets of a tsunami-affected town trying to make children laugh; a female psychologist who visited camps and hugged people, including men; and the construction of toilets without repairing the damage done to people's homes. In such a milieu, it therefore became urgent and imperative for the gap to be closed between how people's needs were being *conceptualized* and how they were *understood* by those at the receiving end of the interventions. A *psychosocial* approach that would focus on the constant interplay between the *inner world* and the *external environment* of individuals seemed to be particularly appropriate in the context of conflict and disaster (PADHI, 2009).

These discussions also reflected the growing emphasis within international development on promoting wellbeing and improving people's quality of life. As discussed in the introduction to this book, the argument that traditional economic development indicators provided only a partial idea of development, and that broader human and social indicators that measured the quality of life and the wellbeing of individuals and communities were needed, had encouraged a multidisciplinary approach within development.

Those involved in the PADHI programme recognized that the promotion of 'wellbeing' underlies an integrated approach to complex emergencies. They argued that, although not always explicitly stated in policy and programming documents, development and humanitarian interventions ultimately aimed to improve the wellbeing of individuals, families, and communities. Therefore, greater conceptual clarity on what 'wellbeing' really meant was needed.

The PADHI programme was established to strengthen the capacity of academics and practitioners in Sri Lanka to clarify local understandings of 'wellbeing' as well as concepts such as suffering and distress, and to incorporate these within development and humanitarian interventions. More specifically, the programme had the following objectives:

- to develop a conceptual framework for understanding the determinants of wellbeing in Sri Lanka;
- to develop methodology and tools to assess wellbeing among individuals and communities through which psychosocially sensitive interventions could be developed.

Box 4.1 Conceptual clarity – what is a 'psychosocial' intervention?

Understanding conflict as a mental health emergency resulting in widespread trauma among affected populations has been widely critiqued (Ager, 1999; Bracken, 1998; Galappatti, 1999; Summerfield, 1996, 1999). Proponents of 'the psychosocial approach' have argued that responding only to the psychological dimension of individual suffering is grossly inadequate; it is imperative to recognize the social dimensions of people's experiences, and to understand how suffering is culturally mediated (Ager, 1999; Honwana, 1999; Jareg, 1996; Lawrence, 1998; McCallin, 1996).

Sri Lanka has a long history of development and humanitarian interventions due to its 'Third World' and 'developing nation' status. These interventions became more significant from the early 1980s onwards with the protracted ethnic conflict that continued until 2009. It became evident during this time that individual-focused therapeutic interventions were not always adequate and were often inappropriate in the context of poverty. Broader interventions – including providing shelter and economic support, skills building, and mobilizing and strengthening social networks – were also recognized as being important in alleviating distress. Many organizations working on mental health in Sri Lanka thus focused not only on the psychological, mental, and emotional dimensions of people, but also on their social relations and material conditions (Galappatti and Salih, 2006). Programmes ranged from medical and therapeutic interventions to livelihood support, from interventions that combined counselling with microcredit schemes for women to setting up play centres for children (Galappatti, 2003; CHA Psychosocial Forum, 2007). These interventions were termed 'psychosocial', and 'psychosocial interventions' became part of humanitarian responses as well as of long-term development programmes.

However, the use of the term 'psychosocial' in describing interventions identical to conventional development programmes, for example the provision of health services, microcredit, and skills training, meant that it was becoming increasingly difficult to differentiate between a psychosocial intervention and a development programme. The blurring of boundaries resulted in a number of debates among practitioners in Sri Lanka on 'what constitutes a psychosocial intervention' (Galappatti, 2003; CHA Psychosocial Forum, 2004). After concluding several mapping exercises of the so-called psychosocial sector, many argued that the type of intervention did not differentiate a psychosocial project from other types of programming; rather, it was the *principles and values* underlying the design of a programme and the *way* in which it was implemented that determined the 'psychosocial-ness' or 'psychosocial sensitivity' of an intervention (PADHI, 2009). Although there was an implicit understanding that being 'psychosocially sensitive' meant adapting a more holistic 'person-centred' perspective, the sector struggled to articulate clearly what principles and values should underline a psychosocial intervention.

Phase I: developing a conceptual framework for wellbeing

Literature review

The conceptual model for wellbeing in Sri Lanka was drafted after a multidisciplinary survey of local and international literature that focused on aspects of wellbeing, wellness, and quality of life, especially within a development context. To identify the key dimensions of wellbeing and human flourishing, the PADHI programme undertook a literature review of local and global understandings of wellbeing as evident in research studies, policy documents, and various state and non-state initiatives that purport to promote or measure wellbeing. The survey looked into how various discourses, theories, and concepts explicitly, or more often implicitly, conceptualize the wellbeing of individuals and communities. A survey of local ethnographic literature and popular cultural practices was undertaken to capture local understandings around wellbeing. In addition, the framework for wellbeing reflects the concepts and theories prevalent in several major discourses, including mental health, mainstream development theories, the discourse on gender and development, and the emerging discussions on elderly people and people living with disabilities.

Focus group discussions

Exploratory fieldwork was then undertaken with the aim of answering the following questions:

- How do different groups of people in Sri Lanka conceptualize, understand, and articulate psychosocial wellbeing?
- What do people in Sri Lanka think promotes or prevents their experiencing psychosocial wellbeing?
- What importance do people give to the identified domains?
- Are there other domains that people feel constitute psychosocial wellbeing, and, if so, what are they?

Fieldwork was conducted in the districts of Hambantota (south) and Ampara (east) with six communities that were affected by the tsunami, the conflict, or both. Altogether, twenty group discussions were conducted; they included Muslim, Sinhala, and Tamil communities. The discussions centred on understanding how wellbeing was conceptualized at individual, family, and community levels. In order to understand how people conceptualize psychosocial wellbeing, the discussion focused on the following themes:

- Current sense of wellbeing: What things are you happy or content with now?
- Aspirations: What are your hopes for the future? What do you desire in order to lead a good life?
- Factors contributing to their current sense of wellbeing.
- Factors preventing the achievement of wellbeing.

Because people are usually reluctant to talk about their personal lives, especially in a group setting, the set of questions based on the above themes first focused on the community, then the family, and finally the individual. For example:

- *Community:* When you think about your community or village, there may probably be certain things that you are happy about, things that you feel positive about. What are those things?
- *Family:* In thinking about your family leading a good life, there may probably be certain things that you are happy about now, things that you feel positive about now. What are those things?

- *Individual:* When you think about an individual, there may probably be certain things that you think are important and necessary for that person to do well and to feel good about life. What are those things?

The findings from this phase of fieldwork were used to ascertain to what extent the framework was useful in capturing the ways in which different communities described wellbeing. The findings also led to the modification of the framework, to reflect local understandings of wellbeing in both design and content.

Phase II: the PADHI framework

The proposed framework for wellbeing is conceptualized as having three key dimensions (PADHI, 2009):

- The **first dimension** attempts to define what **constitutes** wellbeing. It identifies key elements that contribute to a person's or community's overall experience of wellbeing. The framework proposes that psychosocial wellbeing comprises five interconnected domains.
- The **second dimension** identifies what **mediates** the experience of wellbeing. The framework argues that power and influence, and also identity, play a fundamental role in determining a person's achievement of wellbeing, and mediates a person's experience of wellbeing.
- The **third dimension** points to the need for an **enabling environment** if wellbeing is to be achieved. It identifies systems and institutions as key to contributing to or undermining the achievement of wellbeing.

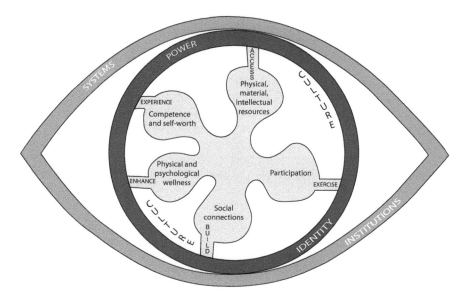

Figure 4.1 PADHI psychosocial framework

The three dimensions of the framework are based on the principle of social justice, which will be discussed later in the chapter. In placing social justice at the centre of its rationale, the framework attempts to address the discrimination, inequity, and disempowerment that influence people's experience and negotiation of everyday life in Sri Lanka.

The framework asserts that an individual (or family or community) experiences wellbeing when they are able to:

- *access* physical, material, and intellectual resources;
- *experience* competence and self-worth;
- *exercise* participation;
- *build* social connections;
- *enhance* physical and psychological wellness.

Emphasis is placed on the active verb in each domain to underscore the importance of agency in achieving wellbeing. The presence of these various elements in a community – resources, opportunities to participate, social networks – does not automatically mean that individual members are experiencing wellbeing. These have only the potential to facilitate the experience of wellbeing; in order to actually experience wellbeing, an individual or community has to have the ability, opportunity, and freedom to actively engage in achieving these domains.

For example, the presence of a school does not necessarily mean that a child is able to go to school. The lack of financial resources to buy books, or the need for the child to stay at home and look after younger siblings, may mean that he or she cannot access the school. Young graduates may have acquired the skills and knowledge to gain employment, but the lack of viable employment opportunities in the community may mean that they are unable to experience competence through the use of their knowledge and skills.

Defining psychosocial wellbeing: the domains

Accessing valued **physical, material, and intellectual resources** refers to natural, material, and educational resources needed to fulfil basic human needs, such as food, shelter, and health. It also points to resources needed to pursue human aspirations, such as education and livelihoods. We draw a distinction between basic needs and human aspirations. Meeting aspirations is about having the necessary skills and facilitating people's desire to plan for their and their family's future. We use the term 'valued' to emphasize that

---

Access to resources usually dominates discussions around wellbeing in Sri Lanka. Economic security meant having an adequate income to meet present needs; having savings to meet future needs and unforeseen expenses; and avoiding debt. Education and employment were thought to determine the degree and quality of economic security. Employment was seen as the primary means through which needs were met. Therefore, the availability of viable livelihood and income-generation activities were stressed so that people could earn an income that met the needs of their family.

different cultural settings and societies may value different types of resources to fulfil their basic needs and aspirations.

Experiencing **competence and self-worth** is the ability to function in society and fulfil roles and responsibilities. This domain points out that individuals must have the opportunity to use their abilities, skills, knowledge, and creativity in their day-to-day life if they are to experience a sense of competence. Competence is also experienced when individuals are able to make informed choices about their own and their family's lives.

> Both men and women experienced competence when they were able to develop a good character. Moral qualities included showing love and compassion to others, belief in oneself, and having a positive life philosophy. Competence was also experienced when people were able to fulfil their duties and responsibilities to family, and they were able to exert influence over their community and country.

Exercising **participation** refers to the opportunity for individuals to have a voice and to shape and influence decisions that impact on their lives. Participation provides a space for self-expression; leadership and participation in politics; and the practice of social, religious, and spiritual rituals. Participation also means influencing decision-making processes at family, community, and even national levels. Participation is one of the fundamental ways in which people exercise their agency and, therefore, is linked to the second dimension of the framework – the exercise of power and influence. Within a development context, the domain of participation recognizes that human beings are not passive recipients or beneficiaries, but are active agents in shaping their own destiny. In emphasizing participation as essential for wellbeing, the framework underscores the principle of self-worth. It emphasizes that even in collectivist societies, individual needs and aspirations should not be subsumed for the collective good.

> Exercising participation was articulated as the ability to contribute to one's community. Participation is exercised mainly to establish and maintain one's membership in the community, and also to expand one's sphere of influence. Exercising participation was also practised by forming social connections. Being an active member of one's community strengthened community relationships. Participation also contributed to the experience of competence and self-worth, since contributing to one's community was an essential aspect of fulfilling one's role and responsibilities.

Building **social connections** recognizes the importance of relationships to psychosocial wellbeing and human flourishing. The domain acknowledges that individuals are usually embedded in a network of social relations. Relationships are central to our identity and sense of belonging. Individuals build social connections through the formation of various types of relationship with other individuals, families, or various groups in society. Social relations usually facilitate access to resources and also enable the practice of one's cultural rituals.

Enhancing **physical and psychological wellness** stresses that good health is essential to the experience and achievement of wellbeing. Physical and mental wellness is not only absence of illness and disease, but also an overall sense of physical vigour and psychological capacity that enables the achievement of the other four domains. Psychological capacity encompasses both cognitive and emotional development. Physical and psychological wellness enables people to actively engage in the achievement and experience of wellbeing. At the same time, people can engage in actively enhancing their state of physical and psychological wellness.

Power as mediator: the role of power, influence, and identity in mediating wellbeing

The PADHI psychosocial framework for wellbeing asserts that power and influence are central to the experience and achievement of wellbeing in Sri Lanka (see Prilleltensky et al., 2001). The framework for wellbeing, therefore, does not define the domains of wellbeing simply as the existence of resources or competencies, or as opportunities to participate and have social connections, but rather it emphasizes the active role individuals, families, and even communities must play in achieving these characteristics. Individuals or communities need to access resources, experience competence and self-worth, exercise participation, and build social connections if they are to experience wellbeing. The interplay between a person's ability and the external environment is mediated by how much power and influence a person is able to exercise, which in turn is determined to a large extent by that person's identity.

The degree to which an individual can exert power is intrinsically tied to their identity. One's given identity as a woman, or as a member of an ethnic minority, or as an economically disadvantaged person determines how much influence an individual can or is allowed to exert in their family and community. A person's identity is an amalgamation of several different components, including gender, ethnicity, class, caste, educational level, and socio-economic status. No single aspect of identity can be said to determine the exercise of power and influence. Depending on the context, one or more of these components may become more prominent than the others. For example, in Sri Lanka, a man's sense of safety and security is intrinsically tied to his ethnic identity. A young Tamil man will not experience the same sense of safety and security going through a military checkpoint as a Sinhalese one.

In the fieldwork conducted, it was clear that power and influence were gained mainly through social networks. It was significant that establishing and maintaining alliances with state officials and political patronage were important sources of influence for all communities. State officials dominated the list of important actors in people's lives. Power gained through social networks facilitated a person's ability to access resources and determined how much control they had over personal and collective goods and services.

Systems and institutions: the enabling environment

An enabling environment is imperative for the experience and achievement of wellbeing. The framework emphasizes the need for supportive systems and institutions to enable the wellbeing of both individuals and communities. The quality of systems and institutions in a particular society can either enable or detract from individuals' achievement of wellbeing. The economic and political systems of a country have a direct impact on the distribution of resources and who can or cannot access them.

A person can experience competence only if institutions such as schools exist to develop competencies. On the other hand, while schools may help develop competencies, a failing economic system may not provide enough opportunities for people to experience competence and self-worth by engaging in productive livelihoods. Physical and psychological wellness can be maintained only if health services, including clinics and hospitals, are available and accessible. Participation can be exercised only if community-level institutions such as civil-society organizations and political parties exist and if the prevailing political system allows for free association. Social connections are also enabled through institutions such as the family and kinship ties.

A social justice approach to enhancing wellbeing

In the introduction to this chapter, attention was drawn to a discussion among academics and practitioners engaged in the psychosocial sector about the need to define what constitutes a psychosocial intervention. It was pointed out that, rather than the type of intervention, it was the principles and values underlying it that determined such a classification. The PADHI programme attempted to draw out what was being implicitly asserted in these discussions and debates as being fundamental to defining a psychosocial intervention.

Concurrently, PADHI also asserted that the philosophy that guides particular approaches within development and humanitarian work is based on certain sets of values. PADHI proposed that the values that underpin particular interventions need to be explicit and also analysed in relation to the norms, practices, and contexts within which they are implemented.

Box 4.2 A social justice approach

A social justice approach calls attention to issues of discrimination, marginalization, and disempowerment. Its focus is on equity, especially when it comes to the distribution of resources, whether they are material, political, social, or cultural. Thus, the framework that is presented here consciously addresses issues of inequity and discrimination. Including 'power' in the framework means that a discussion on wellbeing cannot ignore the issue, and is compelled to focus on identifying the dynamics of power and influence within a given community and how they determine people's experience of the different dimensions of wellbeing.

During each stage of the research process, a key feature to emerge was the extent to which issues such as discrimination, inequity, and disempowerment influenced people's experience and negotiation of everyday life. For example, youth in Sri Lanka identified injustice in society as a primary cause of youth frustration (Hettige, 2002). A number of studies have highlighted that having the 'right' social connections and patronage politics were important aspects of people's day-to-day lives and heavily influenced people's access to services or resources (Amarasuriya, 2010; Hettige et al., 2005). It appeared that, for many people in Sri Lanka, negotiating the everyday was very much influenced by the extent of power and influence they could wield.

Core principles of the PADHI framework

Within a broader social justice approach, the framework draws attention to the need to recognize the intrinsic value of human beings in addition to acknowledging that social relationships, networks, and alliances are important aspects of people's lives. Recognizing the intrinsic value of human beings means treating people as valuable and worthy not merely because they are useful to their families, communities, or nation, but because of their humanity. It also includes appreciating and valuing the potential that exists in each individual. Interventions that focus on women merely as caregivers or on men as primarily breadwinners have identified only their instrumental value. Such a focus does not acknowledge that women and men can flourish in their own right, or recognize their diverse needs and interests.

At the same time, the importance of social relationships in people's lives and their experience of wellbeing are evident in the ways in which their lives are organized around groups and relationships, be these within the family or among a larger community of people. Development interventions often impact on these relationships through the creation of new groups and relationships and by changing or influencing the dynamics of existing ones. For example, setting up microcredit groups might create new alliances but also cause further tensions in existing relationships as a result of increased group pressure on each other to repay loans so that each member of the group can benefit. Similarly, child-rights awareness programmes may result in greater vigilance by the community on parental behaviour, thus changing the dynamics between neighbours as well as within the family. Perhaps even because of these risks and tensions, as much as because of the benefits, the importance of relationships in the everyday interactions of people in Sri Lankan communities cannot be ignored. The psychosocial framework for wellbeing that is presented here underlines the importance of understanding this aspect of people's lives.

This point is particularly important because of the potential for conflict that exists in a social justice approach. A social justice approach challenges existing power dynamics and the status quo. There is, as its intent, a strong transformative element. Transformation from a social justice perspective involves the redistribution of power and resources. Such transformation has the potential to create tensions and conflicts since it is unlikely that many powerful and resource-high groups would agree readily to the redistribution that is being sought. This will, very likely, impact on existing relationships and networks. It is important for people's wellbeing that their involvement in such transformative interventions is well informed, prepared, and supported. For instance, development interventions that seek to raise awareness regarding gender discrimination need to ensure that they also provide support when people act on that awareness. As has been the experience in Sri Lanka, bringing women into decision making has caused conflict with other groups even while benefiting women in general and in particular situations. A social justice approach needs to recognize the transformative potential of conflict but also be adequately prepared to deal with its consequences.

Finally, the framework recognizes that both values and relationships are embedded within a cultural context. It is important that development initiatives understand the cultural dynamics within a community and develop appropriate means to engage with them. The engagement with culture that is being proposed here includes awareness of the diversity and dynamism of that culture among individuals and in communities. For instance, it appreciates the difficulties of identifying one monolithic 'Sri Lankan' culture. Instead, it proposes that development practitioners need to understand the resources and benefits as well as the tensions and conflicts that are part of the dynamic nature of culture. Development practitioners need to ensure that respect for culture does not mean inadvertently reinforcing and reproducing oppressive cultural values. For example, the religious or 'cultural' festivals a particular community consider important may reflect the power of particular types of cultural identity. If development practitioners are unaware of the ways in which such identities are contested or debated, they may inadvertently reinforce and reproduce cultural identities in a way that increases the marginalization of certain groups within a community. This is demonstrated in the way in which NGOs responded to public protests conducted by residents of the Eastern Province against women NGO workers about a year after the December 2004 tsunami. The influx of NGOs in the Eastern Province had resulted in the recruitment of many local women as staff. The protestors claimed that the NGOs were a corrupting influence because these women were discarding what was considered 'appropriate cultural attire' in favour of more 'Western' clothes, and also that women's increased mobility was compromising their reputation. The NGOs responded by asking women to gain permission from their families to continue work, and also imposed the sari as the culturally appropriate dress for local women.

Using the framework: objective setting

Using the PADHI wellbeing framework, a tool was developed that could assess the wellbeing of individuals and communities according to their own definitions and priorities. The PADHI wellbeing assessment tool is a lengthy questionnaire comprising both quantitative questions and qualitative discussions. In implementing it in four communities in rural Sri Lanka, rich data was gathered on people's current sense of wellbeing. However, the process of implementing the survey beyond a research setting was thought to be unfeasible by organizations because it required substantive investment in time, labour, and financial resources.

However, many organizations have used the framework to map and evaluate how their programmes and projects address wellbeing.

Contribution to psychosocial wellbeing

Row 1 assesses the identified and selected needs for the project in comparison with the domains of the proposed psychosocial framework (i.e. each identified and selected need will be recorded in the table under the corresponding domain of the framework). This section looks into what needs arose from the community and which domain of the framework would correspond to those needs. This will enable the organization to identify the particular domain of the framework that is of significant importance for the wellbeing of the particular community (e.g. some communities may emphasize the development of schools and training institutions, which corresponds to the domain of experiencing competence and self-worth; another community may emphasize the importance of building social networks within the community, which addresses the domain of building social connections).

Row 2 assesses the overall objectives of the specific project that is being assessed. Here, the overall objectives are to be recorded according to which domain of the framework each objective corresponds to.

In the same way, **row 3** discusses and explores specific project objectives. Both these steps are about mapping the focus and intentions of the project through the psychosocial framework in order to identify and assess which domains of the framework will be addressed by which objective of the project. This particular mapping activity will also indicate how close (or disparate) are the needs expressed by the community and the final project objectives (i.e. whether the project objectives match the emphasis and prioritization of the community's needs).

Row 4 is for specific activities. The analysis of those activities looks at whether they are designed to:

- meet the needs identified in the initial needs assessment;
- meet the programme's overall objectives;
- meet the specific objectives of the project.

The first three rows indicate the prioritization of the community's needs, and the objectives of the project. Thus, mapping the project activities according to the domains will show how the activities address the project's overall and specific objectives as well as the community's needs. It will help

Table 4.1 How to map using the PADHI framework

	Access to resources	Experiencing competence and self-worth	Exercising participation	Building social connections	Enhancing physical and mental health
Identified **needs** from the initial needs assessment correspond to:					
Overall programme **objectives** correspond to:					
Specific programme/project **objectives** correspond to:					
Activities that relate to:					

recognize the community needs and project objectives that are addressed or completely ignored in the development of project activities.

Identifying appropriate interventions: some key questions

This section is intended to help development planners use the information gathered from the wellbeing assessment and analysis tools to identify appropriate interventions to improve people's wellbeing. A series of questions was formulated to assist in the planning process. The questions are also intended to draw out the underlying principles and rationale for intervention.

1. Identifying the issues and priorities of the community

a. What are the main priorities of this community?
b. What domains and dimensions do they identify as being the most important?
c. How satisfied are they with each of the areas (domains and dimensions)?
d. What are the frequently mentioned issues for each of these areas?

2. Identifying potential beneficiaries

a. What specific groups in the community are experiencing these issues as problems? (For example, older women, young men, widows, families with less income).
b. What are your reasons for choosing one particular group or focusing on one set of issues?

Table 4.2 An example of a completed framework

	Access to resources	Experiencing competence and self-worth	Exercising participation	Building social connections	Enhancing physical and mental health
Identified needs from the initial needs assessment that correspond to:	No/lack of roads and public vehicles to go to the hospital	Lack/poor condition of school	No elected local council member to represent the village	No community-based clubs or organization for women or youth	Lack of adequate medical services in the village
Overall programme objectives that correspond to:	Improved infrastructure facilities	Improved educational facilities and services	Improved capacity for political participation	Improved community support systems	Improved community-based health services
Specific programme objectives that correspond to:	To have a motorable road from the village to the nearest town	To provide physical resources for the construction of a new building in the school	To increase the participation of villagers in local government elections	To increase the community's networking facilities and resources	To build capacity to address immediate medical needs
Specific **activities** that relate to:	Building a 25 km long concrete road from point A to point B	Building a computer lab with 10 computers for the village school	Facilitating 5 workshops to identify key actors and state institutions, and to develop strategies to build enduring links	Establishing a sports club for youth in the village	Conducting 5 first-aid workshops with midwives, local healers, and other identified people, and providing a first-aid box for the village

c. Consider the possible alternative groups and issues you could be working with.

d. Are there specific reasons for not choosing them?

e. What are you going to do with equally vulnerable groups that your intervention will not target?

f. Consider the consequences of including or excluding these groups to: a) the community; and b) the organization.

3. Describing specific issues and priorities

a. What are the main issues your intervention is going to address?

b. What are the enabling and disabling factors identified by the beneficiary group?

c. What institutions and services already exist in the community that address these issues?

d. What community-based organizations address these specific issues in the community?

e. Who appear to be the most important people in the community who provide support and assistance?

f. What are the gaps? In relation to the entire community, what systems and institutions seem to be missing for this particular group?

4. Identifying strategies

a. What is the community/beneficiary group currently doing to reduce or overcome the disabling or inhibiting factors?

b. How satisfied are people with the level of power and influence they have?

c. What strategies do people use to gain influence?

d. What can you do to strengthen the institutions and services helpful to the community/beneficiary group?

e. What can be done to strengthen existing relationships?

f. What can you do to reduce or overcome the disabling or inhibiting factors identified by the community/beneficiary group?

g. How do these strategies relate to the core principles of wellbeing?

h. How do these existing strategies and the intended strategies mesh together?

i. Are there any similarities or differences, or even contradictions?

5. Revisiting objectives

a. What outcomes are your strategies aiming to achieve?

b. Consider the psychosocial framework. Where does your intervention fit in?

    i. Domains of wellbeing: which particular domains does the intervention address?

ii.   Power and identity.

iii. Systems and institutions.

c.   Are your objectives in line with the principles of a wellbeing intervention?

6. Identifying principles

a.   Which strategies do you value? Why?

b.   Do any of them promote the principles of wellbeing? How?

c.   Do any of them undermine the principles of wellbeing? How?

Endnote

1.   The chapter is based on reports and publications of the PADHI research project. The author would like to acknowledge the work of Harini Amarasuriya, Maleeka Salih, Mihiri Ferdinando, and Udeni Appuhamilage.

References

Ager, A. (1999) 'Responding to the psychosocial needs of refugees', in M. Loughry and A. Ager (eds), *The Refugee Experience: Psychosocial Training Module*, Oxford: Refugee Studies Programme.

Amarasuriya, H. (2010) 'Discrimination and social exclusion of youth in Sri Lanka', in R. Gunatilaka, M. Mayer and M. Vodopivec (eds), *The Challenge of Youth Employment in Sri Lanka*, Washington, DC: World Bank.

Bracken, P. (1998) 'Hidden agendas: deconstructing post-traumatic stress disorder', in P. Bracken and C. Petty (eds), *Rethinking the Trauma of War*, London: Free Association Books.

CHA Psychosocial Forum (2004) Report of the workshops on 'Challenges of integrating a psychosocial perspective' organized by the Consortium of Humanitarian Agencies (CHA) and the Psychosocial Support Programme, Sri Lanka, 2004.

CHA Psychosocial Forum (2007) *What is Psychosocial? Understanding Terminology in the Psychosocial Sector*, Colombo: Consortium of Humanitarian Agencies (CHA).

Galappatti, A. (1999) 'No more rehabilitation: a new polemic on trauma and recovery in Sri Lanka', unpublished concept paper available from War-Trauma and Psychosocial Support Programme, Colombo.

Galappatti, A. (2003) 'What is a psychosocial intervention? Mapping the field in Sri Lanka', *Interventions* 1 (2): 3–17.

Galappatti, A. and Salih, M. (2006) 'Integrating a psychosocial perspective into poverty reduction: the case of a re-settlement project in northern Sri Lanka', *Intervention* 4 (2): 127–45.

Hettige, S.T. (2002) 'Sri Lankan youth: profiles and perspectives', in S.T. Hettige and M. Mayer (eds), *Sri Lankan Youth: Challenges and Responses*, Colombo: Friedrich Ebert Stiftung.

Hettige, S.T., Mayer, M. and Salih, S. (eds) (2005) *School-to-Work Transition of Youth in Sri Lanka*, Employment Strategy Paper 2004/19, Geneva: ILO Employment Policies Unit.

Honwana, A. (1999) 'Non-western concepts in mental health', in M. Loughry and A. Ager (eds), *The Refugee Experience: Psychosocial Training Module*, Oxford: Refugee Studies Programme.

Jareg, E. (1996) 'Basic therapeutic actions: helping children, young people and communities to cope through empowerment and participation', in M. McCallin (ed.), *The Psychological Well-being of Refugee Children: Research, Practice and Policy Issues*, Geneva: International Catholic Child Bureau.

Lawrence, P. (1998) 'Grief on the body: the work of oracles in eastern Sri Lanka', in M. Roberts (ed.), *Sri Lanka: Collective Identities Revisited*, Volume II, Colombo: Marga Institute.

McCallin, M. (ed.) (1996) *The Psychological Well-being of Refugee Children: Research, Practice and Policy Issues*, Geneva: International Catholic Child Bureau.

PADHI (2009) *A Tool, a Guide, a Framework: Detailing a Psychosocial Approach to Development*, Colombo: Social Policy Analysis and Research Centre, University of Colombo.

Prilleltensky, I., Nelson, G. and Peirson, L. (2001) 'The role of power and control in children's lives: an ecological analysis of pathways towards wellness, resilience, and problems', *Journal of Community and Applied Psychology* 11 (2): 143–58.

Summerfield, D. (1996) *The Impact of War and Atrocity on Civilian Populations: Basic Principles for NGO Intervention and a Critique of Psychosocial Trauma Projects*, Relief and Rehabilitation Network Paper 14, London: Overseas Development Institute.

Summerfield, D. (1999) 'A critique of seven assumptions behind psychological trauma programmes in war-affected areas', *Social Science & Medicine* 48 (10): 1449–62.

Asha Abeyasekera is a lecturer at the Faculty of Graduate Studies, University of Colombo, Sri Lanka. She has worked for more than 10 years as a practitioner and researcher in the development sector, focusing mainly on gender-related issues and psychosocial work. She was one of the lead researchers and programme manager of the Psychosocial Assessment of Development and Humanitarian Interventions (PADHI) project (2006–9). She received her PhD from the University of Bath.

CHAPTER 5

Inner wellbeing: the Wellbeing and Poverty Pathways approach

Sarah C. White and Shreya Jha

This chapter describes the 'inner wellbeing' approach to wellbeing assessment developed by the Wellbeing and Poverty Pathways project. It begins by describing briefly the history, objectives, and achievements of the research. It then introduces the basic thinking behind the approach we used in modelling wellbeing statistically. It closes by describing how the approach can be adapted for use in development practice.

Keywords: subjective wellbeing assessment, monitoring and evaluation, inner wellbeing, wellbeing in practice

Introduction

This chapter describes the approach to wellbeing assessment developed by the Wellbeing and Poverty Pathways (WPP) project.[1] At its heart is the concept of 'inner wellbeing' (IWB), a new approach to subjective dimensions of wellbeing.

WPP is a research project, and as such is a bit different to the other approaches presented in this book, which were developed directly for use in development policy or practice. We therefore begin the chapter by describing briefly the history, objectives, and achievements of the research. We also introduce the basic thinking behind the approach we used in modelling wellbeing statistically, since this may not be familiar to many readers. We close by describing how the approach can be adapted for use in development practice.

Why inner wellbeing?

We developed the concept of inner wellbeing for two main reasons. First, we realized we needed a more limited term than wellbeing itself if we were to have something specific enough to be empirically testable. Our earlier research in the Wellbeing in Developing Countries Research Group (WeD) from 2002 to 2007 (<www.welldev.org.uk>) had approached wellbeing in a

http://dx.doi.org/10.3362/9781780448411.005

Box 5.1 Distinctive characteristics of the inner wellbeing approach

- A multidimensional model of wellbeing, comprising seven domains that span material, relational, and personal factors.
- A new concept of IWB: what people think and feel they are able to be and do.
- Theory and methods based in research undertaken among resource-poor people in countries of the global South.
- An emphasis on how economic, social, political, relational, cultural, and environmental contexts affect people's experience of wellbeing.
- A reflexive, mixed-method approach that combines quantitative and qualitative data collection and analysis with critical consideration of the way the methods used shape the results produced.

---

very comprehensive way, comprising both 'objective' accounts of livelihoods – characterized as 'resources and needs' – and a subjective measure of goals and satisfaction, characterized as 'quality of life' (Gough and McGregor, 2007; Woodcock et al., 2009). Philosophically, WeD saw wellbeing as being made up of three dimensions – material, relational, and subjective – and this laid some important ground for the study of wellbeing in international development (Gough and McGregor, 2007; White, 2010). Box 5.2 uses the example of land to show how material, relational, and subjective dimensions are closely interrelated. In the new WPP, however, our aim was to put the value of wellbeing to the test: how much, if anything, did attending to subjective perspectives on wellbeing add to more established 'objective' factors in explaining poverty dynamics? For this, we needed to separate out how people were thinking and feeling about their lives from how they were doing in more objective (that is, externally observable) terms.

Second, although we wanted to explore subjective dimensions of wellbeing, we planned to develop our own approach rather than just adopt one of the standard ones. This was partly because the standard methods were developed mainly with North American psychology students and we wanted measures that would fit the particular contexts of our research. It was also because we had a different understanding of what subjective dimensions of wellbeing might involve. In particular, we wanted to distinguish our approach from 'subjective wellbeing' (SWB), which – as Chapter 1 suggests – is often linked to quite a limited understanding of happiness as a way to rate success in life. Instead, we wanted to explore how people were thinking and feeling about what they could do or be in different parts of their lives. We also wanted a term that was open to a psychosocial rather than a strictly psychological interpretation, and could reflect the fact that people in the contexts of our research may think about brain, mind, soul, body, and spirit in quite a fluid way.

The prototype for our seven-domain model was the Sri-Lanka-based Psychosocial Assessment of Development and Humanitarian Intervention (PADHI) and their 'social justice approach to wellbeing' (PADHI, 2009; see Chapter 4). To their five-domain model we added two new domains.

Box 5.2 Material, relational, and subjective dimensions of wellbeing: an example

Fertile land is a valuable material resource in agricultural communities. However, this can be realized only when there is sufficient labour to work on it. Labour depends on co-operation between family or community members. People describe the value of land, therefore, in terms of not only how much they have but also whether there are enough people to work during intensive agricultural seasons. Fractured relationships or not having children to inherit the land may diminish the value of the land for them; on the other hand, they may describe their lives as content because they are a large family that works well together. Thus material resources are transformed by social relationships and this interaction in turn mediates the subjective experience of wellbeing.

Wellbeing scholarship reinforced by exploratory work on quality of life under WeD pointed to the importance of close family relationships to personal wellbeing. Other research of ours had shown the close intertwining of religion with wellbeing (Devine and White, 2013; White et al., 2012). We therefore added a domain on close relationships and one on values and meaning.

Figure 5.1 shows our model of wellbeing. The outer circle shows the wider environment in which people are situated. Although we do not assess this environment directly through the inner wellbeing measure, we do recognize that this broader context critically enables or constrains wellbeing, and consider this particularly in the qualitative aspects of our research. For example, in our Zambia field site, conflict with wildlife was a major issue, as were rights over land (see White and Jha, 2013). The star shows the seven domains of wellbeing. These domains could be assessed on a community basis, but so far we have concentrated on the individual level. Each domain has 'objective' observable aspects as well as the subjective dimension of inner wellbeing. For example, social connections can be measured 'objectively' in terms of density of and centrality within social networks, the extent of participation in giving and receiving help and support, and so on. Inner wellbeing measures of social connections might include whether people feel they know important people, whether they feel that their neighbours are supportive, how quickly they feel they get to know local gossip, and so on. While we separate out the domains for purposes of analysis, we recognize, of course, that in practice they often overlap and are closely interconnected. We also see inner wellbeing not as something that people 'have', but as something that happens in the interaction between people and in the relationships between them and the wider environment.

Designing and implementing the survey

The process of designing the survey was intensive, involving more than fourteen weeks of grounding and piloting in the two field sites, as well as long discussion and multiple revisions among the team back at the office. A major

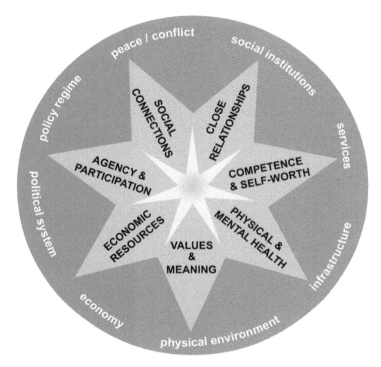

Figure 5.1 The Wellbeing and Poverty Pathways model

concern was length. The longer a survey lasts, the poorer the quality of the data is likely to be. Since most of the people we were talking to had little schooling, the survey had to be administered face to face.

Throughout the process we worked closely with local people – three in Zambia and four in India – on the research team. They acted as peer researchers, mediating, interpreting, and reflecting through the grounding and piloting process and throughout the fieldwork. Talking regularly, both casually and in team meetings, was vital for keeping in touch with each other and discussing what people had learned in informal encounters. It also helped build up researchers' skills, sustained spirits, and meant that we could identify and address any problems at an early stage.

Using quantitative data and analysis to model wellbeing

We have talked above about 'domains', and the statements or questions that we used to assess these, but what does this really mean? Each domain represents an aspect of life that is important to people's wellbeing. As suggested in Chapter 2, you can simply ask people to rate their satisfaction with a domain as a whole – economic status, for example. This has the advantage of being quick and easy, but it doesn't tell you very much. The inner wellbeing approach breaks

---

Box 5.3 Principles and guidelines: designing a survey

- First, only include what you think you will *use*. To include any question, we had to be sure of the work it would do for us.
- Second, don't ask for unnecessary detail that makes answering onerous. For example, if you don't need detailed information on income and expenditure that people find hard (or impossible!) to recall, don't ask for it.
- Third, make the process of doing the survey as conversational as possible. Even in the context of the survey, we wanted to make space for stories and explanations of answers, which would give us a deeper sense of what was really going on for people. This meant taking time at the beginning to introduce ourselves and set respondents at their ease, and ordering questions in a way that would flow reasonably naturally.
- The final principle was perhaps the most important: to pay attention to the way in which people locally were thinking and talking about their lives. At base this is about the quality of listening in any research encounter, which is the foundation of doing research in an ethical way.

---

down each domain into different facets. So, the economic confidence domain might include the facets of immediate sufficiency, longer-term security, having the economic means to participate socially, vulnerability or resilience to economic shocks, and so on. How people rate their position in relation to each of these is important information in itself, and taken together their responses should reflect their economic confidence as a whole. The statistical method for assessing whether different items do indeed belong together so that they collectively make up a domain is known as factor analysis.[2] This assesses whether responses are correlated with each other. In terms of economic confidence, for example, it would assess whether the way people answer about immediate sufficiency provides a good guide to the way they answer about vulnerability to shocks. If so, this suggests that the different items are indeed capturing different facets of a single underlying factor, or domain. Conducting the same procedure across the domains would show that the various domains in turn capture different facets of a single underlying concept, which we have called inner wellbeing. Diagrammatically, this would look like Figure 5.2.

Reflection and adaptation

As mentioned above, studies of subjective dimensions of wellbeing are mainly tested on university students in North America. In trying to transplant an allied method to the very different contexts of rural Zambia and India, we not surprisingly met with a number of challenges (for more details, see White et al., 2013; Marshall et al., 2014; White and Jha, 2014).

Ensuring that phrasing was sufficiently personal could make it uncomfortably direct. Questions about the future were often resisted: 'Who can tell what the future will hold?' Negative statements were also difficult because people feared that they would attract bad luck. In general, people resisted answering direct questions about their own qualities: 'It is for others to say.' They were

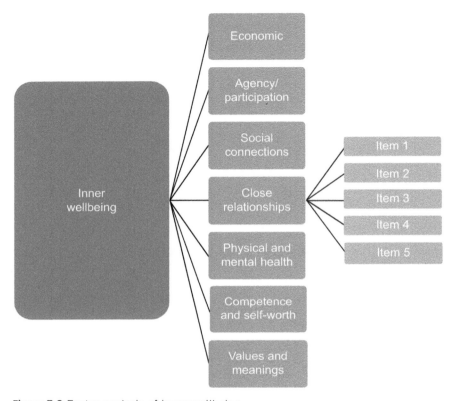

Figure 5.2 Factor analysis of inner wellbeing

also uncomfortable with questions asking them to compare themselves with others. Questions designed to assess self-worth were repeatedly answered in terms of economic capabilities.

Perhaps the most fundamental issue was that people struggled with the character of the questions, which required them to abstract and generalize from their experience. This brought up a real challenge with the factor analysis methodology. The more specific and tangible the question, the easier people found it to answer. At the same time, however, more specific questions carried the danger of going off in many different directions. This could displace the emphasis from what people thought or felt about what they could do or be, and could fail to produce the correlations required by factor analysis! We thus settled on a compromise, agreeing within the team the examples we would give if people struggled with the general and abstract character of the questions we asked, so that everyone would be guided in the same way.

After some experimentation, we settled on five questions for each domain. If there were any more than this, people found them tedious to answer. Any fewer brought problems when we tested for reliability.[3] Similarly, throughout we have stayed with a five-point scale for responses. Reducing it to three did not give us sufficient variability of response, while anything beyond five options was too difficult for people to grasp.

We also thought about the appropriate numerical scale to record responses. Following usual practice, we had begun using a 1–5 scale. This suggests a scale from less to more wellbeing. On reflection, however, we realized that our responses in fact go in two directions, from negative wellbeing (or illbeing) to positive wellbeing. We have therefore converted the 1–5 scale to a numerical scale that reflects this, from –2 to +2. To give an example, the question 'If guests come, do you feel that you can look after them in the proper way?' would give the following answers:[4] 'Very poorly' (–2); 'Somewhat poorly' (–1); 'Neither well nor poorly' (0); 'Somewhat well' (+1); and 'Very well' (+2).

Perhaps the major disappointment was that we failed in our attempts to establish an environment domain. This was not because the environment was unimportant: quite the opposite. In fact, environmental problems were so major for the people in our research areas that they all tended to answer in very similar ways. This is a problem for the kind of statistical analysis we wanted to do, as it needs a range of responses so that you can analyse the variability between people. However, if we undertake follow-up research, we will try again to validate an IWB environment domain. In the meantime, we advocate adding environment to the model for use in project planning and evaluation across objective and subjective dimensions, as set out below.

What have we learned?

It is difficult to sum up in a few sentences the findings of a research project that lasted three-and-a-half years, but some main points are clear.

1. **There is overall a strong positive correlation of inner wellbeing scores with objective circumstances – people who are more advantaged materially and socially tend to have higher inner wellbeing.** People with higher incomes, and especially more land, report higher IWB.[5] Similarly, although the effect is not as strong as that of economic status, married men tend to have the highest IWB scores, with married women next and women heading their own households lowest. This is not true of all individuals or all IWB items, but it is a strong general trend. This was also confirmed in many qualitative interviews, where people talked about the interconnections of peace and happiness at home with economic solvency, for example, or the social and economic marginality suffered by single women. It is also consistent with the main findings of the wider literature, that among poor people at least, economic status tends to be positively correlated with subjective wellbeing scores.

2. **Local understandings of wellbeing challenge dominant models of development and ways of looking at the world.** Each of our research sites had a distinctive local understanding of wellbeing and of relationships amongst people and between people and environment. In our

India research site, for example, the people lived close to the forests, and forest products continued to form an important source of their livelihoods. They have an ecological understanding of wellbeing, in which human community and action, the gift of rain, and the fertility and fecundity of the earth are intimately bound up together. Such conceptions belong to the world of symbol, ritual, and myth, not numbers. But in their vision of a *moral* economy they nonetheless constitute an important resource for building a positive and sustainable future.

3. **Politics matter to wellbeing! The human-centred, whole of life approach of wellbeing has great value in demonstrating the price ordinary people pay for a model of development that prioritizes the profit of a few over the good of the many.** This is especially evident in the Zambia research site, where economic development has undermined villagers' livelihoods, and effective mechanisms for local accountability are lacking. Both quantitative scores and qualitative narratives show that this is associated with high levels of insecurity and low levels of economic confidence and social trust (White and Jha, 2013). By contrast, in our India research villages a strong state policy supporting food security was reflected in people's spontaneous comments that they were no longer hungry, but were now able 'to live our lives'. IWB scores for economic confidence were consistent with this, in the marginal positive range.

4. **Qualitative data and analysis are vital to interpret quantitative measures of subjective dimensions of wellbeing.** Quantitative measures can capture broad trends across large numbers of people, like the correlations between economic and social dominance and inner wellbeing scores noted above. Their full power, however, comes when they are combined with qualitative perspectives. In our research, we, like many others, generally found very high scores for the close relationships domain, way above the overall averages. Does this mean that people are particularly happy with their family lives? This is how some researchers relying solely on quantitative evidence have interpreted such findings. Open-ended qualitative interviews, however, reveal a less happy picture. The high scores reflect what people felt they ought to say, given the central place of family in local ideologies.

5. **Qualitative approaches are also vital if wellbeing assessment is to fulfil its democratic promise.** Quantification depends on large numbers of standard items. This means requiring people to choose from a limited menu of options. You can try – and we did – to make these options as relevant as possible to people's interests and experience, but in the end they are still your options, and they do not allow people to express themselves freely in their own terms. This can be frustrating to the people being interviewed, and uncomfortable for the people doing the interviewing. If you want to understand people's experience and the meanings they make of their lives, they have to be able to put things in their own words.

Box 5.4 Lessons learned

- There is overall a strong positive correlation of inner wellbeing scores with objective circumstances – people who are more advantaged materially and socially tend to have higher inner wellbeing.
- Local understandings of wellbeing challenge dominant models of development and ways of looking at the world.
- Politics matter to wellbeing! The human-centred, whole of life approach of wellbeing has great value in demonstrating the price ordinary people pay for a model of development that prioritizes the profit of a few over the good of the many.
- Qualitative data and analysis are vital to interpret quantitative measures of subjective dimensions of wellbeing.
- Qualitative approaches are also vital if wellbeing assessment is to fulfil its democratic promise.

Adapting the model for use in development policy and practice

Having spent so much time in our research designing and testing a specific set of questions, it is tempting to recommend that they be adopted by others for use in development policy and practice. Chapter 6 describes Traidcraft's experience in producing and using a shortened version of our questions. In general, however, we would be cautious about transplanting a model for research directly into development practice. The logic of research, and particularly the logic of the model arrived at through factor analysis as described above, is quite different to the logic of development intervention. Table 5.1 below sets out various dimensions of this, contrasting two 'ideal types' of wellbeing assessment for research and for development practice, according to five key questions:[6]

1. How does it work?
2. What is it good at?
3. What does it value/aspire to/assume?
4. What is it used for?
5. What are its limitations?

The critical difference is that research seeks to draw from the specific context a 'case' that may shed light on a more general model, framework, or argument. The direction of flow is from concrete and specific to abstract and general. In development intervention, by contrast, the value of a broader framework or model is to deepen understanding of a specific local context. The direction of flow is the reverse: from abstract and general to concrete and specific.

Another key issue concerns participation and expertise. In order to test the model of wellbeing and to analyse the data it produces, you need a reasonable degree of technical knowledge of statistics. It is necessarily an expert-driven model. Part of the logic of pursuing a wellbeing approach, however, is to put people at the centre of the picture. The identification of issues, design of intervention, and monitoring of its effects on wellbeing should therefore be

Table 5.1 Differing approaches to wellbeing assessment

	Quantitative wellbeing assessment research	*Wellbeing assessment for development practice*
How does it work?	• Items as questions or statements generate scores • Correlations between scores used to determine whether items are effective indicators of (more abstract or higher-order) domains/underlying concepts • Correlations between domains used to determine whether they in turn are effective indicators of a yet more abstract or higher-order entity, 'inner wellbeing' *Direction of flow* • Right to left (concrete to abstract)	• Wellbeing model gives organizing template to identify locally relevant items • Not necessarily equal weighting between domains • Interest not in items as revealing domains but in domains as a basis to generate items that reveal something significant about the local context *Direction of flow* • Left to right (abstract to concrete)
What is it good at?	• Simplifying complexity • Reducing complex reality to a more manageable number of concepts/factors • Testing for (causal) relationships • Identifying commonality between people/contexts • Standard tool with minimum needs for adaptation to context	• Revealing complexity • Enabling a '360 degree' perspective • Identifying unexpected impacts/interrelationships • Identifying variability between people/contexts • Localized tool better able to reflect particularities of specific context

What does it value/aspire to/assume?	• Universality • Science/statistical credibility • Simplicity • Abstract/conceptual • Positivism	• Particularity • Local voices • Local relevance/responsiveness • Concrete/embodied • Negotiated meanings
Practical use?	• Pre-practical/academic – legitimating a model that can be used in other ways	• (Partially participatory) project-/programme-level design, monitoring, evaluation
What are its limitations?	• Requires data from large numbers of individuals • Requires sampling to ensure appropriate range of respondents of different types • For analysis, needs significant technical expertise • Standardized form may make for bland or trivial findings	• Requires sensitively guided participatory process • Requires groups organized to give appropriate range of respondents of different types • For analysis, needs skills in critical reflection and understanding of local context • Localized form may limit comparability across contexts

undertaken through a participatory process with local people as the subjects rather than the objects of others' enquiry.

Overall, Table 5.1 indicates that different approaches to wellbeing assessment may reflect very different interests, kinds of expertise, and philosophies of how the world is and how you find out about it. In practice, of course, the distinctions between research and practice may not be so clear. Most obviously, research on wellbeing may be qualitative and have much more in common with the right-hand column of the matrix. However, emphasizing the contrasts in this way is useful in aiding informed choices when selecting your approach.

The remainder of this chapter describes how the IWB approach may be used in development practice.

Inner wellbeing and development practice

There are two aspects of inner wellbeing that are relevant to development practice: the concept, which focuses on what people think and feel they are able to be and do; and the seven-domain model. As an explicit focus for development intervention, the concept of inner wellbeing fits most obviously with psychosocial or empowerment projects that are able to work with people in a quite personal way. These have long recognized the importance of such aspects of inner wellbeing as self-esteem, social cohesion, and supportive relationships (see, for example, Rowlands, 1997). The particular value of inner wellbeing is its strong social grounding in marginalized southern contexts, which balances the dominance of psychology in many psychosocial approaches. Quantitative measures might or might not be useful. What will definitely be important is for the people concerned to identify for themselves whatever markers will serve to chart their progress. More thoughts on designing useful items for quantitative analysis are set out later in the chapter.

Planning for wellbeing in Chiawa, Zambia

This section describes how the seven-domain model might be used to design an intervention. It is based on an exercise we undertook with our research team in our Zambia research site, not a practical experience of project implementation.

The process involves seven stages, and we describe stages one to four:

1. participatory identification of key issues affecting the wellbeing of the community;
2. ordering these by domains;
3. prioritization of key issues for action and monitoring;
4. action plan and identification of indicators (objective and subjective);
5. assessment of the current position with respect to these indicators;
6. action;
7. monitoring and assessment using indicators.

Scoping the issues

People: Facilitator(s); local stakeholders (government and non-governmental organization (NGO) officers, et al.); community groups (structured by key lines of difference, such as leadership position, geography, age, gender).

1. Participatory identification of key issues (separate groups as above)

Process:
- Brief introduction to IWB domains and intention to identify key local issues to help in planning for action.
- Explain that this will bring a fuller range of issues than might be usual in planning a development intervention.
- Explain that this is only an initial scoping of the issues: these will need to be sifted through to determine which can be the target for action.
- Participatory process listing out local problems and priorities (if each issue is recorded as a separate item – e.g. on a Post-it note – this makes the next stage easier).
- Don't worry about classifying issues as objective/subjective, etc.
- If the issues are concentrated in a few domains, use the domain model to prompt for other issues: the close relationship domain, for example, can be useful in bringing out gender issues that might otherwise be overlooked.

Note: There is sometimes anxiety that working in this way will bring up a whole range of issues that cannot be worked on, and will raise expectations that cannot be fulfilled. However, even though we do not choose to work on an issue, it may still be affected by what we do. The example of women in Bangladesh facing increased violence in the home after taking microcredit loans that they passed on to their husbands, and then they had to lobby their husbands to repay, is an uncomfortable reminder of this (see Goetz and Sen Gupta, 1996).

2. Ordering issues by domains (ideally in the same session as identification of issues)

Process:
- Brief revision of IWB domains.
- Assign issues to domains.
- Do not worry if the same issue recurs in several domains; just put it into all of them.
- An additional 'environment' domain should be included.

3. Prioritizing key issues for action and monitoring (this begins in groups, as above, but moves into a whole community meeting, with representation from all the different groups)

Process:
Groups:
- Reflect on the chart produced, showing issues by domain. Pay particular attention to issues that recur across several domains, as their recurrence may suggest that these are the critical ones to work on.

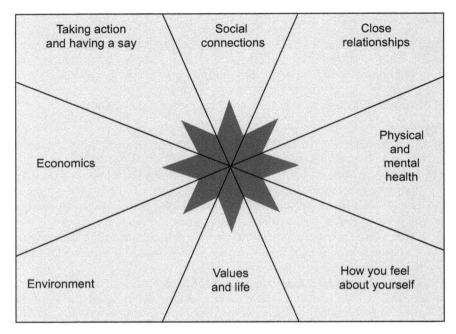

Figure 5.3 Chart for organizing issues by IWB domains

- Identify a maximum of 10 issues as priorities for action.
- Reflect on the resources available – this will affect what is practical to work on.
- Refine priorities to a maximum of five.

Community meeting:
- Ground rules: respect for all.
- Each group presents their priority issues.
- Discuss and identify collective priorities.
- Elect/select an action group to take the issues further.

4. Action plan and identification of indicators (smaller action group)

Process:
- Action group identifies key action that can be taken to address each of the priority issues.
- Action group identifies two indicators, one objective and one subjective, that can ultimately be monitored through a self-managed participatory process.

An example of how this might look in the context of Chiawa, Zambia, is given below. Chiawa is a Game Management Area on the edge of a national park, so some of the main issues that people identify concern their relationship with wild animals, their marginal agricultural livelihoods, and the lack of accountability for community-level resources.

Objective 1:   *Reduce injuries to people by wildlife*
Action: Link to Zambia Wildlife Authority system to monitor, record, and report incidents.
Action: Establish programmes to raise people's awareness of the dangers and how to live safely with wildlife.
Objective: Number of incidents reduced.
Subjective: Improved scores on a question measuring fear of injuries from wildlife.

Objective 2:   *Reduce damage to crops by wildlife (also economic)*
Action: Raise awareness of fencing/lights and other forms of protection.
Action: Increase access to these methods of protection.
Indicators: Amount of crop damage reduced.
Subjective: Improved scores on a question measuring confidence that people will harvest what they have planted.

Objective 3:   *Increase the benefit that people gain from wildlife (also economic)*
Action: Ensure that safari lodges pay tax and that the tax comes to the community.
Action: Ensure that those responsible in the community distribute funds fairly and effectively.
Indicators: Material benefits are seen in the community.
Subjective: Improved scores on a question measuring people's views on the value of wildlife.

Objective 4:   *Increase farming productivity*
Action: Raise awareness of traditional methods of herd rotation, conservation, irrigation methods, etc.
Action: Increase access to the inputs necessary to implement these.
Indicators: People harvesting more/getting better returns on their investment.
Subjective: Improved scores on a question measuring people's sense of control over farming livelihoods.

Objective 5:   *Reinvigorate processes for community level accountability*
Action: Establish a trust with representation from all parts of the community.
Action: Hold regular open meetings to provide information and promote discussion on key community issues.
Indicators: People attend and participate actively in meetings (men and women, older and younger).
Subjective: Improved scores on a question measuring people's confidence that if they speak they will be listened to.
                  Improved scores on a question measuring people's confidence that the community can get together to take action.

Further subjective indicators

It would be possible to stay with the indicators that relate to the areas on which action is to take place directly, as indicated above. Alternatively, a few additional indicators might be included to widen the scope and capture some of the more indirect effects of programmes relating to self-confidence, social trust, and overall sense of wellbeing. These might include, for example:

- How far do you feel you have been able to overcome life's difficulties?
- How far do you feel you are able to help other people?
- How much can you trust people beyond your immediate family to be with you through bad times?
- How well is your family able to co-operate?
- To what extent do you feel that life has been good to you?

Using IWB to track or think through potential impact

Another way in which IWB can be used in development practice is to assist in project monitoring, by thinking through the likely impact – or tracking the existing impact – across the range of domains. Development projects often have a range of impacts on people's lives, only some of which feature in project objectives. Figure 5.4 below shows a chart that can be used to think this through – adapted from a similar chart designed by Wellbeing Wales (see Chapter 11).

The chart sets out the domains and five levels of impact, from strong positive to strong negative. The exercise is best done in small groups to generate discussion. Specific kinds of likely impact are written on Post-it notes and then positioned in the appropriate place on the chart. At this stage there is no need to worry about separating out objective from subjective. It is also useful to think at both collective and individual levels, and about both project participants and those who will become their clients, employers, or customers. It is a useful way of identifying potential unintended impacts and thus to guard against them, or at least to be in a position to monitor them. Again, an eighth domain – which considers impact on the natural environment – will be helpful.

- The first step is to think through the various impacts of the project, both positive and negative.
- The next step is to assess how negative or positive the impact of the intervention is and to write these results into the boxes in the 'Project impact by wellbeing domains' board (Figure 5.4).
- On the wellbeing domains board, the impacts are graduated along a scale from 'Strong positive' (+2) to 'Strong negative' (–2); this indicates the scale along which you can assess the impacts and place them in the slot corresponding to the intensity of their impact in the relevant domain.

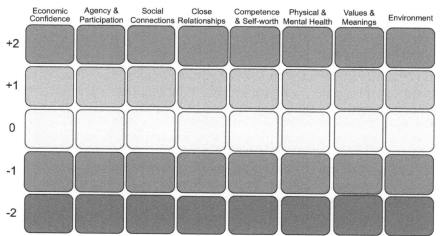

Figure 5.4 Project impact by wellbeing domains

As an exercise, we have used this chart to assess the likely impact of a project run by Care International in association with multinational companies such as Unilever in rural Bangladesh.[7]

Dubbed the 'Avon Ladies' project, this involves poor women selling cosmetics from house to house, in a context where purdah norms value women staying in the home. Using the wellbeing domains board draws attention to a wide range of possible impacts and generates a great deal of discussion. For example, people point out that, while the project enables women to earn an income, the amounts are rather marginal (+1); the women's sense of agency probably increases but their scope for community participation might fall given the increased time they are spending working and travelling (+1 and −1 = 0); it is probably positive for social connections as they will become important news channels for other women who are required by purdah to stay at home (+2); close relationships may be ambivalent in relation to husbands – they may appreciate that the woman is earning but not that she is out and about. There is also the question of who does household duties – is a daughter kept home from school to substitute (−1)? There is likely to be a positive effect on the woman's sense of competence and self-worth (+2); on the other hand, there may be a heavy toll on her health – walking much of the day carrying merchandise in the hot sun (−2). The values and meanings domain raises some interesting dilemmas. There is the local sense that women should not go out, and the tensions the businesswomen may experience regarding their need to go against this. There are also questions at the community level about encouraging spending on cosmetics, especially 'fair and lovely' skin-whitening products, and about the overall economic and social effect of the community as a whole spending more on goods produced by multinationals that no one really needs.

Designing questions

If you do want to use the IWB concept in development practice, designing good questions is key. There are two important things to bear in mind when framing questions: the first is to frame the question in ways that reflect the ways in which people speak about their lives; and the second is that the questions are sufficiently general to be relevant to different groups of people.

Above, we describe our learning and adaptation during the research. This provides a number of pointers for good and bad practice. Box 5.5 gives you an opportunity to try it yourself.

Eliciting answers

A visual representation of the answer scale can be used as an aid in eliciting the answers. It helps people to understand the graduated scale, which is bipolar in nature, with the two ends representing the most negative and most positive answers to each item.

This is easily understood through the set of responses to the question 'If official decisions are made that affect you badly, do you feel that you have the power to change them?'[8] Figure 5.5 illustrates the visual scale with the corresponding scores and answers. As you can see, the scores increase from left to right: on the far left, the two dark circles represent the most negative score of –2; the next single dark circle represents a score of –1; the middle circle is half dark and half light, representing a score of 0 or a balance of negative and

---

Box 5.5 Test yourself!

What makes a good item for quantitative assessment of subjective perspectives on wellbeing?
    This box contains five potential IWB items, all of which are flawed in some way. Take a look at them and see if you can spot the errors! How could you rephrase them to produce a better question? (Answers at the end of the chapter).

1. How far do you either fear or welcome the new road?
2. Are your children able to get a good education?
3. How satisfied are you with the quality of medical treatment you are able to access?
4. How good are you at what you do?
5. (To what extent) do you struggle to make ends meet through the year?

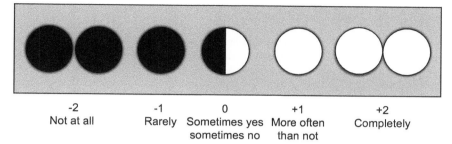

-2		-1	0	+1	+2
Not at all		Rarely	Sometimes yes sometimes no	More often than not	Completely

Figure 5.5 Visual scale with corresponding responses to the question 'If official decisions are made that affect you badly, do you feel that you have the power to change them?'[9]

positive; a single light circle represents a slightly positive score of +1; and two light circles represent the most positive answer of +2.

As this response scale demonstrates, the answers move from an extremely negative point (–2), through a neutral mid-point (0), to an extremely positive point (+2).

Setting goalposts

As mentioned in Chapter 2, the trouble with using subjective indicators in project evaluation is that they are just that: subjective! It is important, therefore, that when undertaking a baseline survey which involves subjective indicators you include qualitative questions that set the 'goalposts' – what the people concerned would consider a –2 or +2 score.

The value of this will be evident when you come back to assess how people's subjective perceptions have changed. It may be that the score is no different or even lower several years on, because expectations have increased (the goalposts have moved). But this could signal project success, rather than failure!

Strengths and limitations

The contribution of IWB to policy is set out above. Here we concentrate on strengths and limitations at the project level.

Strengths

- IWB has been field-tested and validated across differing cultural contexts.
- The framework encourages people to think differently about the issues that concern them.
- The IWB questions, which are rooted in a psychosocial understanding of people, reveal the complexity of their lives and how they understand the relationships between various aspects of their lives. This understanding

offers an insight about what to bear in mind when designing development interventions.

- The IWB domain framework offers a process or approach for assessing the impact of a project in a more comprehensive manner, taking account of the unforeseen effects of an intervention.
- IWB offers a way to generate quantitative scores relating to subjective dimensions of wellbeing for individuals and communities.
- Qualitative information reveals the contexts of people's answers, which help us to better understand the quantitative data.
- It can be used in either an individual or a group process.
- A visual image representing the answer scale can be used to enable people with limited literacy to mark their own answer; it also helps link the idea of a scale with the verbal answers, reducing the effort involved (for the respondent) in having to remember what the answers are.

Limitations

- An IWB approach tends to be time-consuming because of the way it encourages people to think of their lives in the round, including parts of their life that they may not be used to talking about.
- IWB items that will produce useful information for project evaluation need to be generated within a particular context, not taken 'off the peg'.
- Facilitators need to have extremely good people skills. These include the usual skills required to conduct an interview or participatory group process, augmented by an understanding of how to pose and explain questions that are more abstract or personal than those that are usually used.
- They also need the personal skills to be able to respond appropriately if people become upset as the questions recall traumatic events from their lives.
- As with any subjective data, IWB scores cannot of themselves indicate change or project impact. Qualitative data also needs to be used to interpret the scores and assess changes in the 'goalposts', as well as the number of goals.

Box 5.6 The Answers: what makes a good item for quantitative assessment of inner wellbeing?

1. The question goes in two opposite ways, so it is impossible to score. A better alternative would be: 'To what extent do you welcome the new road?'
2. Not everyone has children, and the question suggests a yes/no answer rather than a graduated set of answers. The question is more about the quality of the education available than what it means for the person himself or herself. A better alternative would be: 'How satisfied are you with the education the children in your family are getting?'
3. The question mixes two issues: *access* to treatment and *quality* of treatment.
4. This is a direct question to rate oneself, and people are likely to either answer it very positively or refuse to answer.
5. This is what we describe as a 'closet objective' – it has a strong in-built bias by economic status.

Endnotes

1. Wellbeing and Poverty Pathways is a research project supported by the Economic and Social Research Council and the Department for International Development Joint Scheme for Research on International Development (Poverty Alleviation) grant number RES-167-25-0507 ES/ H033769/1, August 2010 to April 2014. See <www.wellbeingpathways. org> [accessed 19 June 2014] for more details.
2. There are several different forms of factor analysis, but for more details you will need to refer to a statistics textbook.
3. Reliability in statistics is the measure of how closely items within a domain correlate to one another.
4. This is the second of five questions in the economic confidence domain.
5. We did not ask about income directly but used a proxy for this based on main source of livelihood and amount of main crop harvested.
6. The term 'ideal type' does not suggest perfection, but that these are ideas constructed for the purpose of analysis, rather than reflecting directly an empirical reality.
7. For details see <www.theguardian.com/journalismcompetition/ bangladesh-avon-ladies> [accessed 19 June 2014].
8. This is the third question in the economic confidence domain.
9. The visual scale does not have the scores and answers written on it; they have been added here for the sake of explanation.

References

Devine, J. and White, S.C. (2013) 'Religion, politics and the everyday moral order in Bangladesh', *Journal of Contemporary Asia* 43 (1): 127–47.

Goetz, A.M. and Sen Gupta, R. (1996) 'Who takes the credit? Gender, power and control over loan use in rural credit programs in Bangladesh', *World Development* 24 (1): 45–63.

Gough, I.R. and McGregor, J.A. (eds) (2007) *Wellbeing in Developing Countries: New Approaches and Research Strategies*, Cambridge: Cambridge University Press.

Marshall, N., White, S.C., Gaines Jr., S. and Jha, S. (2014) 'Wellbeing assessment in practice: lessons from Wellbeing and Poverty Pathways', in J. Rowley (ed.), *Well-being Ranking: Developments in Applied Community-level Poverty Research*, Rugby: Practical Action.

PADHI (2009) *A Tool, a Guide and a Framework: Introduction to a Psychosocial Approach to Development*, Colombo: Social Policy Analysis and Research Centre.

Rowlands, J. (1997) *Questioning Empowerment: Working with Women in Honduras*, Oxford: Oxfam.

White, S.C. (2010) 'Analysing wellbeing: a framework for development policy and practice', *Development in Practice* 20 (2): 158–72.

White, S.C. and Jha, S. (2013) *The Politics of Wellbeing, Conservation and Development in Chiawa*, Zambia, Briefing No. 2, Bath: Wellbeing and Poverty Pathways. <www.wellbeingpathways.org/images/stories/

pdfs/briefing_papers/Chiawa_BP_final18_Dec_2013.pdf> [accessed 19 June 2014].

White, S.C. and Jha, S. (2014) 'The ethical imperative of qualitative methods: developing measures of subjective dimensions of wellbeing in Zambia and India', *Ethics and Social Welfare*, Special Issue on 'Understanding Well-being in Policy and Practice'.

White, S.C., Devine, J. and Jha, S. (2012) '"The life a person lives": Religion, wellbeing and development in India', *Development in Practice* 22 (5–6): 651–62.

White, S.C., Gaines Jr., S.O. and Jha, S. (2013) 'Inner wellbeing: concept and validation of a new approach to subjective perceptions of wellbeing – India', *Social Indicators Research* <http://dx.doi.org/10.1007/s11205-013-0504-7>.

Woodcock, A., Camfield, L., McGregor, A. and Martin, F. (2009) 'Validation of the WeDQoL-Goals-Thailand measure: culture-specific individualised quality of life', *Social Indicators Research* 94: 135–71.

Sarah C. White is a sociologist of international development and wellbeing working at the University of Bath. She has been researching wellbeing in developing countries since 2002, with a particular focus on South Asia. She directed the Wellbeing and Poverty Pathways project in India and Zambia (2010–14). She received her PhD from the University of Bath.

Shreya Jha is a doctoral student and research officer on the Wellbeing and Poverty Pathways project at the University of Bath. Her work focuses on measuring wellbeing through a mixed-methods approach and on understanding how people's narratives of wellbeing are influenced by their social and relational contexts, and also mediated by the type of research encounter. This builds on her previous experience of having worked in NGOs in New Delhi, India, in the areas of gender, disability, and mental health, with a focus on how to integrate mental health perspectives in mainstream development interventions. She has an MSc in wellbeing and human development from the University of Bath.

Acknowledgements

This work is supported by the Economic and Social Research Council/ Department for International Development Joint Scheme for Research on International Development (Poverty Alleviation) grant number RES-167-25-0507 ES/H033769/1.

CHAPTER 6

Traidcraft: assessing human flourishing

Lizzie Spencer, George Williams, and Liza Stevens

This chapter describes how Traidcraft has collaborated with the Wellbeing and Poverty Pathways project to utilize a survey methodology to assess the subjective 'flourishing' or 'wellbeing' of beneficiaries – how they think and feel. The methodology has been adapted and developed to ensure that it is both accessible to participants with low or no literacy and cost-effective for a small non-governmental organization to undertake. To date, the assessment process has been used as part of project monitoring and evaluation with participants in Bangladesh and Tanzania. The assessments provide quantitative data that forms part of the project baseline – against which changes can be tracked – and qualitative information that contributes to programmatic and organizational learning. The chapter describes Traidcraft's journey from its initial motivation to engage with the wellbeing agenda, to the numerous challenges it has faced and continues to grapple with; these include, for example, sampling, training facilitators, attribution, and adaptive preferences.

Keywords: wellbeing, flourishing, wellbeing assessment, NGO, subjective wellbeing, monitoring and evaluation, low literacy, illiteracy

Introduction

Traidcraft's thinking about wellbeing began around 10 years ago during an organizational strategic review. This review process led to the redrafting of our vision statement as follows: '*A world freed from the scandal of poverty, where trade is just and people and communities can **flourish**.*' Our focus on trade means that income measures will always remain a core indicator of impact for Traidcraft. However, the emphasis on *flourishing* grew from our recognition that increased income is a necessary, but not a sufficient, condition for improving people's quality of life, and that there are important wider dimensions of life beyond the material. In the strategic review discussions that formulated Traidcraft's 2011–14 plan (which included consideration of the *Wholly Living* report: Theos et al., 2010), our board assigned the organization the task of developing a system to assess whether, and how, our work contributes to

http://dx.doi.org/10.3362/9781780448411.006

Box 6.1 Traidcraft

Traidcraft is recognized as one of the UK's leading fair trade companies. In addition to Traidcraft plc, our trading company, Traidcraft also consists of Traidcraft Exchange, a development non-governmental organization (NGO). Our two halves work in complementary ways to further the organization's overall mission – making markets work for the poor. Our work revolves around three interrelated areas:

Trade: facilitating access to local, regional, and international markets for small enterprises.
Support: building the capacity of poor producers to trade effectively, helping them form enterprises and collaborative groups and equipping them with business skills.
Influence: challenging injustice and encouraging changes in government policies, corporate practices, and public attitudes to trade, development, and poverty.

---

improve flourishing. The aim was both to prove our impact and to improve our practice.

Our approach to assessing flourishing developed in several stages. The first stage involved focus-group discussions with small groups of project participants in three countries: India, Bangladesh, and Kenya. These discussions focused on the questions 'What do you need for your life to be good?' and 'What does flourishing mean to you?' In their answers, many participants emphasized the importance of income, but other factors were also identified as being crucial. These crossed many dimensions of life, including: free choice and control over your life; dignity and self-esteem; education and new skills.

These conversations were crucial in helping us ground our thinking in the values and opinions of our project participants. However, we felt that this grounding needed to be complemented by a coherent conceptual model that could organize these interacting dimensions, and that could be practically and consistently utilized within Traidcraft's monitoring and evaluation (M&E) processes. Our search for such a model led us to the Wellbeing and Poverty Pathways project, led by Dr Sarah White at the University of Bath.[1]

The model of inner wellbeing developed by the WPP was both aligned with Traidcraft's conception of 'flourishing' and applicable within our programme work. We decided to adopt the model and to base our assessment methodology on the WPP survey approach. In order to make the survey approach practical, affordable, and useful for us at a project or programme level, some adaptations were made to the approach.

Adapting the Wellbeing and Poverty Pathways model and methodology

Traidcraft worked collaboratively with the WPP team to adapt their individual (one-to-one) survey methodology to make it suitable for our purposes.[2] We had two interlinked requirements that needed to be met.

Firstly, we needed to conduct the assessment in the most efficient way possible – while balancing the need to have data from at least 100 respondents for the quantitative analysis to be credible. Here, efficiency refers to both the monetary cost of conducting the surveys and the time required from our

---

Box 6.2 The inner wellbeing model

'Inner wellbeing' seeks to capture 'what people think and feel they are able to be and do' (White et al., 2013). The model consists of seven interrelated domains from which wellbeing is derived. They constitute the seven points of the star in Figure 6.1. Aspects of the wider environment enable or constrain wellbeing: these are included on the outer circle surrounding the star (see Chapter 5 for more information on the model).

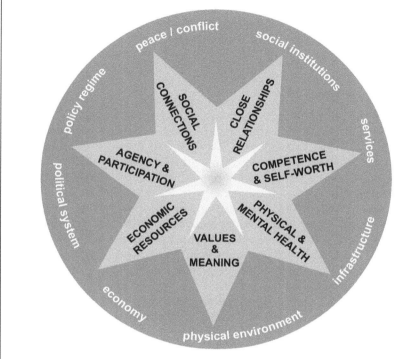

Figure 6.1 The inner wellbeing model

---

project participants. Secondly, the survey needed to be made accessible to people with low levels of literacy or who were not literate at all. The following adaptations were made to the assessment methodology to make it fit with these requirements:

- The survey process was adapted so that it could be administered with small groups of respondents at a time. Each survey respondent completes his or her own survey, but the whole group is guided through the process by a facilitator.
- The original survey consisted of 38 questions: five questions for each of the seven domains, plus three general review questions. The original survey was too time-consuming for our purposes, so it was reduced to a 'mini-survey' of 19 questions.[3] The questions included in this survey

were selected by the WPP team on the basis that they offered the best statistical results, i.e. those that indicated that they were both addressing the underlying concept of the domain and eliciting a range of answers.
- The survey was adapted so that participants with low levels of literacy could complete it on their own. The survey facilitator reads out each question in turn and the possible answer options. The answer options are accompanied by a visual key that is included on each participant's copy of the survey. The facilitator refers to the images in the key while explaining the answer options. Participants are then able to mark on their own the answer that best matches their own feelings or thoughts.

Piloting and implementation

Following the adaptations described above, the new group-based mini-survey was initially piloted with groups of textile producers in Rajasthan and Delhi in India in the first half of 2012. The pilots provided us with positive feedback on the viability of assessing individual wellbeing with a group-based methodology, on the strength of the questions being reliable measures of wellbeing domains, and on the experience of the overall process.

After further refinement, Traidcraft and our project partners utilized the group-based assessment methodology to conduct a full-scale baseline survey in September 2012 for a new project launched with smallholder farmers in Bangladesh. A total of 114 project participants were surveyed in groups comprising five or six people. Again, the feedback we received from participants on the methodology was very positive.

In November 2013, after having further refined the group-based survey from our experience in Bangladesh, we used it as part of the project baseline for a

Figure 6.2 The mini-survey in progress in Bangladesh, September 2012

new project working with beekeepers in Tanzania. We surveyed 118 project participants, this time in groups of 10 to 12. In addition, we introduced a focus-group discussion after the survey to generate further qualitative data and learning. See the case study in this chapter for a detailed description of this process.

Traidcraft's group-based survey methodology

Our aims

Traidcraft's aim is to understand the impact of our work on individual and community flourishing. We want to find out *what* has changed, but also *how* Traidcraft's project activities might have influenced this change in both positive and negative ways. We want to *prove* impact, but also *improve* our practice. By implementing assessments at baseline and end-of-project stages, we aim to gain an indication of project participants' wellbeing and how it has changed over the project period.

Overview

Our methodology has evolved through practice: what follows is a description of the latest iteration, used recently in Tanzania. In essence, the methodology involves a three-stage process repeated with small groups of participants.

Process

As mentioned above, the survey is conducted with groups, but completed individually by participants. Each group survey is administered by a team of two trained facilitators who sit with the participants in a circle. One facilitator leads the process. He or she starts by using a standard introduction to the survey, explaining the reasons for doing it, and summarizing the process they will follow.

Each participant is given a paper copy of the questionnaire on which they mark their own responses. Pencils, pens, and coloured stickers are available for them to use. The lead facilitator reads through the wellbeing questions

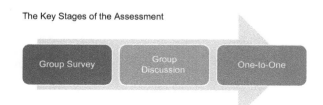

The Key Stages of the Assessment

Group Survey   Group Discussion   One-to-One

Figure 6.3 Traidcraft's three-stage survey process

that constitute the main section of the survey. He or she explains each one using a standardized, locally appropriate explanation. After each question, the lead facilitator explains the five possible answers available, referring to the visual key that illustrates these (see Figure 6.4 below). A large-scale copy of the visual key is used as a visual aid to support the process (as seen in Figure 6.2). Participants then mark their answer in the appropriate box.

During the process, the other facilitator observes the group's reaction to the survey and supports the process as required. The facilitator's observations are recorded on a standard form that includes specific questions to prompt reflection.

Following the completion of the wellbeing survey, participants are requested to complete the demographic information requested. Facilitators support those participants who cannot read or write.

Once all the participants have completed the demographic information, facilitators initiate an informal discussion with the participants still seated in the circle. They discuss the following issues with them:

- How was the experience of completing the survey?
- How were the questions? Were any particularly easy or difficult to answer?
- What factors are currently affecting people's wellbeing in your community?

We have two aims at this stage. Firstly, we aim to give participants the opportunity to share their feedback on the survey. We have found that many participants are engaged by the survey and want to share their views on it – many report never having been asked these kinds of questions before. Secondly, we aim to gather further (qualitative) information on how participants understand wellbeing and what factors affect it. A facilitator records all the key points mentioned.

Following this group discussion, one participant is selected to participate in a one-to-one interview. In advance, the project team will have selected the key questions they wish to focus on in the interview that relate to key project outcomes. In an indirect manner, the facilitators invite the participant to share their reasons for answering these questions the way they did. Their responses are recorded. Our aim here is to deepen our understanding of why participants are answering the way they are and to ascertain whether our programmes have had an impact on their lives.

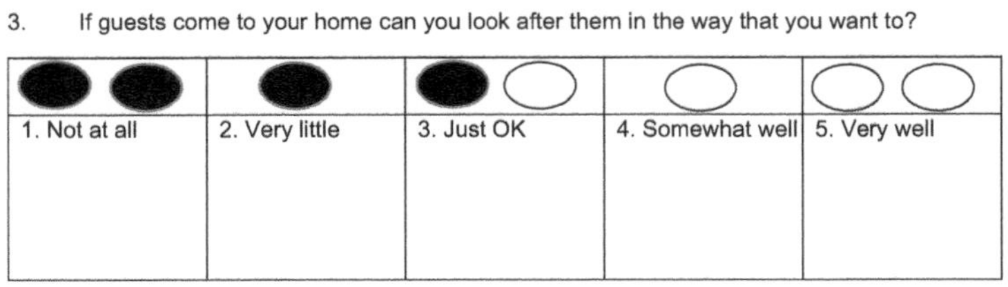

Figure 6.4 Visual key used in the Traidcraft survey

Following the survey in Tanzania (November 2013), we have decided not to include one-to-one interviews in the baseline survey as we found that they did not add significant value to the qualitative data generated by the focus group discussions. We may use them for the end-of-project surveys and are looking to integrate the wellbeing questions in interviews for participant case studies as part of our normal ongoing project M&E activity.

Survey

The survey questionnaire has two sections:

- Section 1 covers participants' basic demographic data. This section is filled in *after* the completion of section 2. This is because participants with low literacy levels will need support from facilitators to complete section 1, making the process difficult for everyone to achieve at the same pace.
- Section 2 is the wellbeing survey itself. There are now 16 questions on the survey: each is answered on a one-to-five Likert scale. Thirteen questions assess participants' inner wellbeing across six of the seven domains (two or three questions per domain). The remaining three questions are general review questions.

Following our survey in Bangladesh and discussions with the WPP team, the close relationships domain has been dropped from the survey, as it has proved impossible to gather meaningful data on this domain.[4]

To help low-literacy participants navigate their way through the questionnaire, and to assist the facilitators in ensuring that all participants are following together, two key amendments have been made to the presentation of the survey:

- Only three questions are printed on each page, which enables the facilitator to easily explain to participants which one they are currently referring to: top, middle, or bottom.
- A unique, locally appropriate page identifier symbol is used on each page. Facilitators can refer to this rather than to page numbers (see Figure 6.5 below).

4.   If you say something do people listen to you?

Kama ukisema jambo lolote, je watu wanakusikiliza?

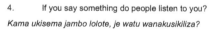

1. Never	2. Very little	3. Sometimes yes, sometimes no	4. More often than not	5. Always
Kamwe	Kidogo sana	Wakati mwingine wananisikiliza wakati mwingine hawanisikilizi	Mara nyingi wananisilikiliza	Daima/ muda wote

Figure 6.5 Example of a page identifier at the top right-hand corner

Information generated and analysis

The following outputs are generated by the whole assessment process:

- quantitative data from each participant on 16 wellbeing questions, which is accompanied by key demographic information (e.g. gender, age, marital status, education level);
- notes on the facilitators' observations on each group's reaction to the survey questions and process;
- notes on key points made by participants during the group discussion;
- notes on each one-to-one interview respondent's explanations of their answers to five or six key questions.

The quantitative data generated by the survey is transcribed into Excel (and/or SPSS). First-level analysis generates average scores per question and average scores per domain (see Figure 6.6 below). These can be disaggregated by demographic variables. The data spread can also be assessed, for example by standard deviation. Further analysis can assess whether differences are significant in statistical terms.[5]

Analysis of both the qualitative and quantitative information should be conducted by members of the project team – those who have been involved in conducting the assessment. The process of analysing the information generates useful questions and points for further discussion. We feel that this process itself is as useful as any final written report.

Use of information

To date, Traidcraft has used the full assessment methodology only as part of two separate project baselines. Until we have completed the corresponding assessments at the end-of-project stage, it is impossible to assert the precise value of the information generated. However, the two full assessments, plus the initial pilots, have generated useful learning.

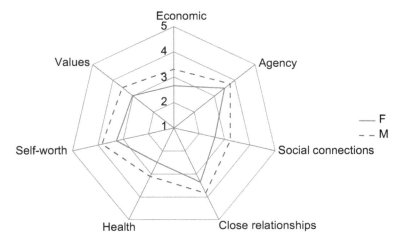

Figure 6.6 Spider diagram depicting average scores per domain by gender (data collected from smallholder farmers in Bangladesh)

Reporting on project impacts. The qualitative and quantitative information gathered through the assessment process will contribute to our reporting on project outcomes and impacts. This may be used for funding and comm-unications purposes, to give donors, supporters, and trustees an indication of changes in project participants' wellbeing over the course of the project. Although it will be difficult to attribute any change in wellbeing to Traidcraft's interventions absolutely, associations can be identified.

Testing assumptions and highlighting areas for attention. The information may also help test our project assumptions and highlight aspects of project design that require further attention. Our recent assessment with beekeepers in Tanzania brought to light the low levels of trust between group members and, related to this, their negative experiences in the past of group marketing ventures. This provided the project team with useful new information about the viability of a planned project activity around group collection and marketing centres.

Reflexive practice and organizational learning. The assessment process provides a new forum in which project teams can engage with project participants. The project team in Tanzania reports finding this useful as a potential starting point from which to continue discussions with project participants on both project-specific issues and wider concerns related to the context in which the project is implemented. We hope that these will generate useful organizational learning as well as promote more reflexive practice. This process should continue as the project team participates in analysing the information generated by the assessment.

Highlighting opportunities for action. Strengths and limitations may be identified through the process, which in turn could lead to useful collaborations with other organizations that provide specific services beyond the scope of Traidcraft's work. In addition, feedback provided by participants who have undertaken the assessment suggests that the process of self-reflection prompted by the survey questions is, in and of itself, useful to the participants. One participant reflected that 'I liked the survey because it is important to evaluate my own life', and another said that 'the answers are within ourselves'. Participants and survey facilitators have suggested that this process could provide a basis or impetus for further community or group planning and action. Sharing and analysing the information generated by the assessment with project participants could further enhance momentum in this regard.

Using the methodology: lessons learned

The whole process of developing and using the group-based wellbeing assess-ment methodology has been a positive learning experience for Traidcraft. This section provides advice for practitioners considering using this methodology, as well as highlighting some remaining issues and dilemmas.

Resources

Developing and piloting the survey methodology has been resource-intensive. In addition, implementation itself requires a considerable time commitment from the field staff involved, reducing time available for other project activities. Alongside time, potentially significant costs are incurred when bringing the survey teams together for training and then transporting them to different locations to conduct the assessments with different groups. It is important not to underestimate the financial and human resources needed to produce useful outcomes.

Translation: ensuring local understanding of the questions

The importance of translating the questionnaire into appropriate local language and idioms to reflect local ways of thinking cannot be overestimated. It is advisable that programme staff play a central role in this process. In recent consultations with our staff in East Africa, for example, issues with the following question were identified: 'To what extent do you feel that luck has been in your favour?' The concept of 'luck' was considered to be inappropriate in rural Tanzania, due to negative connotations with gambling. The term 'blessed' was deemed appropriate and the wording of the question adapted accordingly.

Selecting facilitators

Whether survey facilitators should be project staff members or external consultants is a matter we have debated at length. With field staff as facilitators, there is the potential for relationships with project participants to be strengthened through this new form of interaction, and for relevant learning to be captured. However, one could also argue that using project staff to conduct these assessments increases the likelihood of biased responses, thereby compromising the objectivity of the information recorded. In our view, the most important consideration is the quality of the facilitators' group-process skills.

Training facilitators

Training facilitators is an important part of utilizing the methodology. Our training has been in the form of a residential workshop conducted over two-and-a-half days. The aim of the workshop is to provide facilitators with an understanding of the wellbeing framework and the aims of the assessment, and to equip them with the group-work skills necessary to conduct the assessments effectively and consistently. The training is very practical and enables the facilitators to take ownership of the survey process.

Sampling

How representative the assessed sample of project participants needs to be is another important consideration. In Bangladesh, we balanced the need to be representative in our sample against the simple issue of logistical convenience – both ours and that of the project participants. Although our sample may not be as representative as academic standards would require, on a practical level this was deemed to be 'good enough'.

In addition, it is important to decide at the start of the process whether you intend to survey the same group of participants at baseline and at the end of the project. If you do, attrition needs to be factored into planning and the original sample needs to be large enough to accommodate this – bear in mind that your end sample needs to include over 100 respondents for the quantitative analysis to be reliable.

Group dynamics

Group size is another key issue for consideration. We feel that anything larger than 10 to 12 may be too difficult for facilitators to manage. During the group surveys, some level of discussion is inevitable. While this may raise concerns about the extent of undue influence between participants, we feel that these discussions can be constructive if managed well. The facilitators' training highlights their role as 'facilitators', not as controllers: they are encouraged to emphasize that the survey is about what participants think and feel *individually*, rather than prohibiting discussions in a heavy-handed manner.

Location

Ideally, the survey location should be as 'normal' as possible for participants, which may mean outside in village courtyards or in communal meeting places. In our assessments in Bangladesh, the group surveys were characterized by a general lack of privacy: other community members observed and commented throughout the process. It is not always possible to provide a private space for participants, and it may not even be desirable, as it could be perceived as preferential treatment and contrast with local ways of interacting. Instead, facilitators should be prepared to respond appropriately if they feel that there is too much intervention from outside observers.

Travel

Ideally, respondents should not have to travel long distances to participate in the assessment. Apart from the time expended, it may also result in participants not feeling that they have a real choice in participation once they have arrived. It is also important to consider weather conditions and harvesting seasons: these may affect ease of travel and also have ethical implications, because the assessment might take participants away from their normal daily activities.

Cultural and religious influence

What people feel able to be and do is often guided by strong cultural and spiritual beliefs. How to understand wellbeing while taking into account the beliefs and social expectations that guide individuals is an ongoing matter for Traidcraft. For example, in Bangladesh, many participants used the term 'Inshallah' ('if Allah wills it') when discussing their capability to make changes to their lives. In addition, responses to questions about the close relationships domain are strongly influenced by beliefs about how families *should* be. As a result, we have decided not to include the close relationships domain in our surveys.

Ethical considerations

Although to date Traidcraft has minimal experience of this, we are aware that there is the potential for participants who are experiencing difficult circumstances to become upset due to the personal nature of the survey questions. It is advisable that strategies are in place to support those who may become distressed. Moreover, the process may prompt participants to voice and request solutions to community problems they are experiencing. Providing solutions to these may be beyond the organization's remit and capacity. It is advisable in these cases to listen to concerns and make referrals to other services where possible.

Strengths and limitations of the methodology

Strengths

Adaptability. The framework is easily adaptable to different contexts. The model has been statistically validated in developing-country contexts after extensive fieldwork by the WPP team.

Data and information. The assessment involves a mixed-methods approach, producing both quantitative and qualitative data. This increases the richness of the information collected, strengthening our understanding of the wellbeing of our project participants.

Participants' experience. Participants report that they enjoy taking part in the assessment process. They say that the survey is a new experience for them and that they have not been asked these kinds of questions before. There is an empowering aspect to participants marking their own responses on the survey.

Building project staff skills and M&E capacity. The involvement of field staff in the assessment process helps develop their group-process skills. It has the potential to increase their capacity to work with and to build relationships with project participants. It helps them to develop a better understanding of the project context and to learn from the participants. In addition, it encourages a stronger sense of their ownership of the project's M&E processes, potentially increasing the project team's understanding of project impacts and their role within that.

Limitations

Resources. As discussed previously, the investment of human and financial resources is significant. Traidcraft's process is being adapted continuously to increase cost-effectiveness.

Data and information. Using mixed methods for the assessment presents challenges when it comes to combining, collating, and using the information generated. In addition, the value of qualitative information collected is contingent upon the quality of the relationship between the facilitators and the respondents, the facilitators' skills, and the time devoted to exploring issues in depth. Without investment in these factors, the research encounter may be counterproductive and the information inadequate. Also, analysis of qualitative data can be time-consuming and complex: the usefulness of information is limited if analysis is done superficially.

Attribution. Whether any change in participants' wellbeing can be attributed to Traidcraft's activities is questionable. As we know, wellbeing is influenced by complex and interacting circumstances. However, the inner wellbeing framework provides a structure with which to understand the interplay of factors, including how these may have interacted with Traidcraft's intervention. Survey questions could be adapted to make them specific to project activities, which would increase our ability to attribute change to Traidcraft.

Moving goalposts. Changes in individuals' aspirations may make comparing findings between the baseline and end-of-project assessments difficult. As conditions improve, people's expectations also change. This challenge may make the collection of 'objective' data appear more attractive. However, we feel that the challenge of understanding people's moving goalposts should be embraced as a way to truly understand the process of development. One way to do this might be to define key parameters with assessment participants at the baseline stage, for example by asking them to explain and agree on what a 'five' and what a 'one' look like for each question. These ideas and visions can then be referred to again when conducting the survey at the end of the project.

Reception and buy-in. As mentioned in the introduction, Traidcraft's wellbeing journey has been stimulated at various key junctures by our board. In this and other respects, the process has been mainly UK-led. We feel that it is important for international organizations to recognize that, while discourse around wellbeing and flourishing has become relatively common in the UK context, this is often not the case in the areas where our work is focused. We have encountered some well-founded scepticism on the part of many of our overseas colleagues and partner staff regarding our attempts to measure our project participants' wellbeing. They have questions around, for example, the 'validity' of the information generated, how useful it can actually be, how costly it is to collect, and the extent to which teams' focus is being taken away from actually doing something about evident *illbeing* to asking people questions about it. We have to acknowledge that at present we don't have satisfactory answers to all these questions. While there can be no simple recommendations on how to enhance buy-in, we feel that acknowledging the newness of the endeavour and communicating clarity of purpose – why we want to do it and how we think it will help – are important and too easily overlooked.

Ways forward

For Traidcraft, the process of developing our methodology to assess flourishing has been both challenging and enriching. We are still in the early stages of our journey and thus far attention has been focused very much on the development of a practical assessment methodology. Until our baseline assessments are complemented by the corresponding end-of-project assessments, we remain unsure of exactly how valuable the approach is to our work. We look forward to grappling with this issue on the next stage of the journey. Meanwhile, and as interest in the area develops in the international development community, we are keen to share our learning with others with whom we share the aspiration of finding better ways to understand and ultimately improve the wellbeing and flourishing of poor producers.

Case study: wellbeing assessment in Tanzania

Beekeepers Economic Empowerment Tanzania (BEET) is a Traidcraft Exchange project working with 2,760 beekeepers across two regions of Tanzania. It builds upon our previous successful work with beekeepers in Tanzania and Kenya. The BEET project supports the formation of beekeeper groups and provides apiculture training to help improve honey quality and quantity. It facilitates links between the beekeepers and skilled service providers, as well as to markets and buyers. In November 2013 we conducted a wellbeing assessment as part of the project baseline. This was our second full-scale wellbeing assessment.

The process

- Over two-and-a-half days we met with 118 project participants in single-sex groups of 10 to 12 at a time. These survey groups were formed from the beekeeper groups and they met at their usual group's meeting location.
- Groups were surveyed by teams of two facilitators who were introduced to our assessment methodology during a two-and-a-half-day practical training workshop. Three of the survey facilitators were project staff and five were independent enumerators.

- Each assessment lasted an average of around two-and-a-half hours. This included the facilitators' introduction to the process, the group survey, the group discussion, and the individual interview conducted with just one group member.

Following learning from our pilot assessment in Bangladesh, which had generated a lot of valuable quantitative data but very little useful qualitative information, we increased the focus on gathering qualitative information – both in the assessment methodology itself and in the training workshop. As mentioned before, we introduced the group discussion step between the survey itself and the one-to-one interview. Our primary aim was to offer the participants the opportunity to share their thoughts on their experience of completing the survey – in Bangladesh, a lot of participants did this, but we had not properly planned for it. By formally integrating it into the assessment process, we hoped to capture feedback from participants and use this to inform future assessments. Our secondary aim was to deepen our understanding of what factors are currently affecting people's wellbeing within our project areas: the data from the survey tells us how people are feeling, but not why. We hoped that information gathered during this stage would address this gap.

An important development introduced during the training workshop was the adaptation of this 'focus group' stage into what we termed 'Sodas and Group Discussion'. This may sound like a minor change, but we found it to be an important one. No matter how much emphasis is given to the relaxed nature of the exercise during the facilitators' introduction, a certain formality remains when sitting in a circle with a pair of strangers, ticking boxes on a printed form. The sharing of sodas helps break the ice once the surveys have been completed. Group discussion questions are then introduced in as conversational a way as possible. The primacy of 'sodas' in the title 'Sodas and Group Discussion' is intentional.

For the one-to-one interviews, the project team chose to focus on key survey questions they felt would potentially have a significant impact on the success of the project, but that do not get explicitly measured within the formal logical framework-based M&E system. The questions chosen focus on self-confidence, ability to bring about change with others, and ability to face troubles that arise in life. The key objective of the one-to-one interviews is to understand *why* participants are answering the way they are. However, direct 'why' questions can appear critical or even confrontational, so the facilitators choose to approach the issue more indirectly by asking the participants, 'What thoughts were going through your mind as you answered this question?'

Our survey sample

A total of 118 people participated. Of these surveys, five were not completed fully and their results were removed from the analysis. Of the 113 'valid' surveys:

- 57 were completed by women and 56 by men – these include married, divorced, single, and widowed men and women;

- 45 men and 46 women had attended some primary education; 4 men and 5 women received some secondary education; while 6 men and 6 women had no formal education;
- the age of participants ranged from 20 to 80 years;
- all of our participants were Muslims, except for one Christian.

Our sample was large enough to do some disaggregation by gender, but any attempt at further disaggregation (for example by marital status, age, or education level) would have resulted in samples that were too small for us to draw meaningful conclusions from them.

Initial analysis of quantitative data

In this section we present only an overview of the information obtained by the survey process. More detailed data analysis is available on request.

Overall, we see that our mean scores per domain cluster around the mid-point of 3 – neither positive nor negative (see Figure 6.7). The agency and participation domain has the highest average score (3.64), while 'physical and mental health' has the lowest (2.72).

When we disaggregate this by gender, noticeable differences start to appear for the following domains (see Figure 6.8):

- *Economic resources*: mean score for men = 2.71; women = 3.20.
- *Competence and self-worth*: mean score for men = 3.38; women = 3.10.

Further analysis using SPSS reveals that these differences are statistically significant.[6]

Analysis with SPSS reveals statistically significant differences between men and women in response to the following questions.

We should perhaps be aware that the clustering of scores around the mid-point (3) may suggest that people are answering by sitting on the fence! We certainly hope that this is not the case. Standard deviations for the domains suggest a variation in how people are answering. In addition, the qualitative information indicates a very positive response to the survey and real engagement with it on the part of the participants. Until we complete the final survey at the project end and see whether any changes occur, it will be very difficult to make the final assessment on this issue.

Initial qualitative analysis: group discussions

- In the group discussions, all groups reported feeling very positive about participating in the survey. Several fed back that they found the questions easy to understand and liked how they were focused on their personal lives. Several commented on how it was a useful process for them to reflect on these issues.
- When discussing factors that are currently affecting people's wellbeing in their communities, issues of environmental degradation and change

Table 6.1 Traidcraft survey questions

Question code	Domain
Economic resources	
Economic 1	How well would you say you are managing economically at present?
Economic 2	If guests come to your home can you look after them in the way that you want to?
Agency and participation	
Agency 1	If you say something do people listen to you?
Agency 2	How confident do you feel that (along with others) you will be able to bring about change?
Social connections	
Social connections 1	Do you have contacts with people who can help you get things done?
Social connections 2	How much can you trust people beyond your immediate family to be with you through bad times?
Social connections 3	If something happens in your area when do you get to hear about it?
Physical and mental health	
Health 1	How much do you worry about your state of health?
Health 2	How often do you feel stressed?
Competence and self-worth	
Self-worth 1	How well have you been able to face the troubles that have come so far?
Self-worth 2	To what extent do you have confidence in yourself?
Values and meaning	
Values 1	How far would you say you have peace in your heart at the end of the day?
Values 2	To what extent do you feel that life has been good to you?
General review questions	
How happy	Taking all things together, how happy would you say you are these days?
Past 12 months	Considering the last 12 months, how well would you say you are doing money-wise?
Five years ago	Comparing your standard of living overall now with five years ago, how would you say you are doing?

were mentioned repeatedly. Specific issues included deforestation, climate change, and droughts. Environmental sustainability is an area that is not explicitly covered in the survey but with which the project engages, making this information pertinent to Traidcraft's work with the beekeepers.

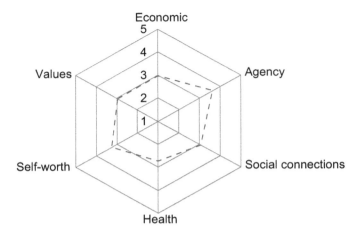

Figure 6.7 Mean score per domain, Tanzania

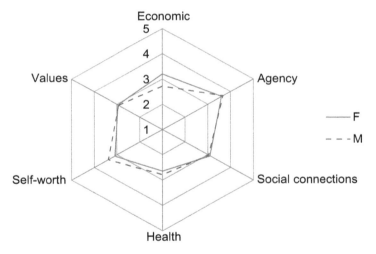

Figure 6.8 Domain mean scores disaggregated by gender, Tanzania

- Challenges relating to setting up and running businesses were also mentioned repeatedly. These included specific issues such as lack of capital and limited access to markets. These are issues that the project is specifically focusing on, so in this way the information coheres with the original assessment of the need for the project. These issues were mentioned by both men and women. The quantitative data (as discussed above) suggests that the issue is more of a concern for men than for women.
- In addition, two of the groups described a previous group-marketing venture that failed due to some corruption. This has resulted in a lack of trust and may have implications for future planned project activities around group marketing of honey.

Table 6.2 Domain mean scores disaggregated by gender, Tanzania

Domain	Question	Mean score: women	Mean score: men	Comment
Economic resources	If guests come to your home can you look after them in the way that you want to?	3.54	2.70	The statistically significant difference between how men and women perceive their economic resources – women more positively than men – is driven by this question.
Social connections	How much can you trust people beyond your immediate family to be with you through bad times?	3.07	2.68	While there is no statistically significant difference between men and women for the social connections domain as a whole, two of the three questions that make up the domain reveal noticeable differences between men and women.
Social connections	If something happens in your area, when do you get to hear about it?	2.51	3.07	It would seem that, in effect, these differences cancel each other out.
Competence and self-worth	To what extent do you have confidence in yourself?	3.32	3.71	While the difference between men and women for this domain is not significant in statistical terms, on the two questions relating to this domain, there is a significant difference in how men and women answer this question.
General review questions	Taking all things together, how happy would you say you are these days?	3.18	2.63	Further analysis indicates a strong correlation between how people answer this question and the economic resources domain.
General review questions	Comparing your standard of living overall now with five years ago, how would you say you are doing?	3.47	3.05	Comparing the overall average scores (women and men), people are more positive about their present situation compared with five years ago than when assessing the situation over the last 12 months.

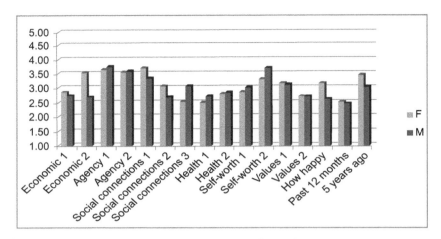

Figure 6.9 Mean scores by question and gender, Tanzania

- Conflict between arable farmers and livestock farmers, as well as between farmers and pastoralists, was also mentioned repeatedly.
- Poor-quality health services were also mentioned as a concern by two of the groups, which coheres with the survey results in which the health domain has the lowest mean score (women and men) at 2.72. For women, this domain has the lowest mean score (2.65), and it has the second-lowest for men (2.79; only the economic domain scored lower at 2.71).

Initial qualitative analysis: one-to-one interviews

- When asking people to explain more about their feelings of confidence to bring about change (survey question 5), it is notable that five of the 10 people interviewed referred to having been part of other organizations, committees, and groups and gaining experience and confidence through those experiences. This may reflect a bias in our selection of participants for the one-to-one interviews, but at the same time it gives some credence to Traidcraft's project methodology that supports the formation of producer groups.
- In addition, while question 5 forms part of the agency and participation domain, the responses from participants illuminate the connectedness and overlap between domains. Several people referred to how their own ability to analyse situations gives them confidence (overlapping with 'competence and self-worth') and how seeking advice from others also gives them confidence (overlapping into 'social connections').
- When asking people to explain their feelings about how well they have faced the troubles that have come so far in life (question 11), the answers given were quite diverse but, again, the ability to analyse situations and

seek help from others was mentioned, as well as having belief in oneself and being able to plan well.

> 'I liked the survey because it is important to evaluate my own life.'

- Interestingly, money and one's economic situation were mentioned by four of the interviewees (three men and one woman) when explaining their responses to question 11 and/or to question 12, which is about having confidence in oneself. The message from these people is that when they have money they can face the troubles that come their way and/or that it gives them confidence in themselves. This may come as no surprise, but it again provides further credence to Traidcraft's focus on economic empowerment.
- Finally, it is interesting to note that two of the five women interviewed mentioned how managing their households well and making decisions within that arena provides them with confidence in themselves. This may be a useful counterbalance (or addition) to the view stated above about the importance of money for bringing about feelings of confidence.

Initial outcomes

The BEET assessment enabled Traidcraft to test key refinements of our methodology, including improved cost-effectiveness through working with larger groups, introducing the 'Sodas and Group Discussion' process, and focusing the one-to-one interviews on key survey questions. The additional emphasis placed on collecting qualitative information has certainly added texture to the analysis. Whether sufficient quality qualitative information has been generated is a matter of ongoing discussion.

The team enjoyed conducting the assessment process and participating in the training workshop. Project staff felt that the assessment has enhanced their understanding of the beekeepers with whom they are working. Specifically, the importance of understanding the impact of environmental degradation has been strongly emphasized through the process, as has the need to consider amending certain project activities around group marketing in light of the participants' recent bad experience in this area and the resulting lack of trust. Moreover, the project team considers the whole process to be the beginning of a 'conversation' with the project participants that will continue throughout the life of the project and enable more informed project implementation.

Endnotes

1. Henceforth referred to as the 'WPP'.
2. More specifically, Sarah White, Shreya Jha, and Shweta Verma (an independent consultant) from the WPP were instrumental in this process. Traidcraft's gratitude to them for their hard work, patience, support, and flexibility is extended here.

3. Nineteen questions were piloted and then utilized in our first full-scale assessment in Bangladesh in 2012. This was reduced further to 16 questions for our Tanzania assessment conducted in November 2013.
4. See Chapter 5 on the WPP for further information.
5. More advanced statistical analysis can be used to bring out directions of influence and suggest predictors of wellbeing.
6. Many thanks to Andrea Baertl Helguero for her support with this.

References

Theos, CAFOD and Tearfund (2010) *Wholly Living: A New Perspective on International Development*, London: Theos.
White, S.C., Gaines Jr., S.O. and Jha, S. (2013) 'Inner wellbeing: concept and validation of a new approach to subjective perceptions of wellbeing – India', *Social Indicators Research* <http://dx.doi.org/10.1007/s11205-013-0504-7>.

Lizzie Spencer worked with Traidcraft during 2012 and 2013, testing the utility and feasibility of integrating wellbeing assessments into their monitoring and evaluation systems. Her interest in developing assessment tools to understand wellbeing developed when studying for an MSc in wellbeing and human development from the University of Bath. Lizzie has also worked for and volunteered with social justice organizations, including Christian Aid and Voluntary Services Overseas (VSO). Currently, Lizzie works for a city farm that provides recreation, education, and therapy using food, farming, and the environment as themes to improve individuals' wellbeing and help overcome isolation.

Liza Stevens is currently Head of Programme Funding and Evaluation at Traidcraft, where she has worked for the last 14 years in a number of different roles, including East Africa Programme Manager. Prior to Traidcraft and her current career in international development, Liza worked for over 15 years in the UK arts sector (theatre, dance, and visual arts) in a variety of marketing, fundraising, and management roles. She has an MA from the University of Edinburgh and an MBA from the Open University (UK).

George Williams is a member of the Traidcraft team that has been exploring how to integrate wellbeing assessment into the organization's monitoring and evaluation processes. His work has focused on training trainers, coaches, and mentors. George has a strong interest in organizational learning and supporting people to do what they do better. He recently completed his MSc in wellbeing from the University of Bath, where his dissertation focused on exploring the impact that adopting a wellbeing approach has on the work of development organizations.

CHAPTER 7

CAFOD: quality of life Batteries Tool

Harriet S. Jones

The Batteries Tool is a participatory quality of life (QoL) assessment that is adaptable to varying contexts and does not require high literacy skills or complex training. QoL is an important outcome measure for international development and public health programmes supporting people living with HIV. In this context, measures are often complex, narrowly health-focused, and do not reflect on other factors that have an impact on QoL. Using the Batteries Tool for HIV programme monitoring supports a broader understanding of QoL and considers it across four domains: health, psychosocial, human rights, and livelihoods. Monitoring complex outcomes such as QoL is possible in resource-constrained settings and has benefits beyond programme monitoring. Discussions on QoL can be empowering for individuals, support a more client-led approach to programming, and help programmes identify their contribution or where there are gaps in service provision or support.

Keywords: quality of life assessments, quality of life, HIV, CAFOD batteries tool, outcome measure, HIV programmes and services

Introduction

The quality of life (QoL) Batteries Tool was developed by CAFOD staff and partners as a simple participatory tool for individuals to assess changes in their QoL. The version of the tool described in this chapter was developed specifically for CAFOD-supported HIV programmes, for use by people living with and affected by HIV engaged in these programmes.

In an era of effective HIV treatment, individuals with access to the right treatment, care, and support can live long and healthy lives. With appropriate support, disease progression is delayed and life expectancy for people living with HIV dramatically increased. This has resulted in a shift from supporting individuals with critical end-of-life care to enabling them to live full and happy lives. In this context, QoL has become an important outcome measure for HIV programmes and services.

http://dx.doi.org/10.3362/9781780448411.007

Box 7.1 CAFOD

The Catholic Agency for Overseas Development (CAFOD) is the official Catholic aid agency for England and Wales. CAFOD works with more than 500 partners worldwide to end poverty and injustice. CAFOD works with people of all faiths and none.

CAFOD has worked as part of the global HIV response since the mid-1980s. A vital component of this response has been CAFOD's holistic approach to HIV-related care, support, and mitigation, and its goal to improve the QoL of those living with and affected by HIV. CAFOD defines this holistic response as one that goes beyond supporting only health to include psychosocial and spiritual support, and support to address human rights and livelihoods security. This programme approach prompted questions on not only what constitutes a holistic response, but also how to measure improvements in QoL.

Measuring the effect of this support has meant moving away from simply considering declines in HIV-related mortality to demonstrating the positive contribution that HIV care and support interventions make in people's lives. This type of measurement not only is suitable for donor reporting, but also addresses the need to be accountable to individuals and communities, and ensures that responses are suitable to their needs, sensitive to the contexts in which they live, and ultimately are effective.

Too often evaluation approaches and tools are top-down, donor-driven, require complex data analysis systems and technology, and are administered by professionals with clients as passive recipients. The findings they elicit are often far removed from the lives of those they are intended to affect. More importantly, these types of assessment leave little room for individuals to have a say in what is important to them, nor do they allow people to influence changes and support in their own lives.

The Batteries Tool attempts to address these issues and enables individuals and groups to identify what they perceive to be components of a good QoL and assess changes in these over time. The tool helps identify individual challenges as well as the broader trends reported by programme clients, and whether these changes can be attributed to programme interventions or whether they are beyond the control of the programme. This enables programme staff to recognize the contribution a programme makes in people's lives, assess challenges and gaps, and adapt the programmes accordingly.

The Batteries Tool

The tool described in this chapter is based on the concept of 'batteries'. Individuals are asked to reflect on their energy levels or 'how full their batteries are' across specified domains of their lives. Although the tool can be used to measure QoL across a range of development programmes, this chapter will talk about the tool as it has been developed specifically for the HIV programmes that CAFOD supports.

A 'full and happy life' – or, in other words, a good QoL – will mean different things to different people and will be dependent on a person's history and

---

Box 7.2 Developing the Batteries Tool

The idea of the Batteries Tool was initially conceived by Clodagh Byrne – a CAFOD staff member who worked with CAFOD partners in Cambodia to assess changes in the QoL of programme clients, and to increase participation of clients in programme monitoring and design. CAFOD's HIV partner – Cambodia HIV/AIDS Education and Care (CHEC) – had applied other QoL measurement tools and had resorted to expensive external evaluations, but saw the need for a measurement tool that was simple, participatory, and adaptable, and also reflected the reality and contexts of people's lives.

CAFOD's HIV programme partners in various countries in Africa were facing similar challenges. At the same time, CAFOD required evidence that its own programmatic approach was having beneficial effects on clients' QoL. Programme partners across various countries needed a tool that produced useful and useable information and did not require complex or time-consuming data management systems and analysis. The tool needed to be both practical and useful for the partners' purposes and to be easily understood and applied by those who the programmes were trying to reach.

Around the same time, CAFOD's multi-country HIV team, meeting in Nigeria with a selection of programme partners, did extensive work to identify areas that comprised a comprehensive, holistic HIV care and support response, from which four domains were identified: 1) health; 2) psychosocial and spiritual support; 3) human rights and legal support; and 4) economic and livelihood security. These became the domains both to map service provision against a holistic model, and to determine changes in the QoL of clients over a given time frame.

A combination of these two pieces of work resulted in the development of the Batteries Tool as an effective means of assessing QoL changes in the context of HIV care and support programme responses. The domains have been used as a set framework to allow for a standardized approach to monitoring CAFOD's HIV care and support programmes. Programming across these four domains – normally by partners working in collaboration with other local service providers – is what CAFOD sees as constituting the holistic response needed to improve the QoL of people living with and affected by HIV.

Initial versions of the tool were piloted in 2008 with a number of programme partners in Cambodia, Kenya, Ethiopia, Nigeria, and Mozambique. It was then adopted as the standard QoL monitoring tool for CAFOD's HIV care and support programmes in 2010.

---

the context in which they live. Factors that make one person happy and fulfilled may not have the same effect on another. The Batteries Tool and its development reflect this ethos: the tool does not ask specific questions or impose preconceived ideas of what it means to have a good and happy life on those completing it.

The concept behind the tool is that the energy levels in batteries provide a good way of representing QoL; the more components that an individual has to make up a 'full and happy life', the higher the energy levels of their batteries. The energy levels are considered for the four separate domains, represented as four separate batteries. Through this conceptual framework, the tool looks at:

- what it means to have a good QoL;
- how an individual's QoL has changed over a period of time;
- the reasons for this change (and attribution to the programme);
- implications that this may have for the future.

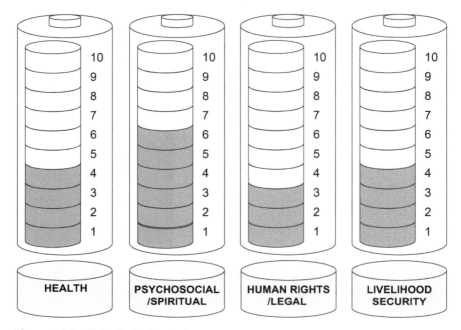

Figure 7.1 CAFOD's batteries tool

What makes a good and happy life?

Before considering any changes in QoL, it is useful to ascertain what QoL means in a specific context and to different people. Breaking down the concept of QoL by asking what it means to have a full and happy life will reveal components that are applicable to different individuals or in a specific community, and will also familiarize participants with the concept of QoL. This is the initial and probably most important stage of the process and is simply done by asking participants (usually in a group setting) to generate ideas on *what components they need to lead a good and happy life*. Components may include good health, a loving family, good friends, support from friends, faith and an accepting place of worship, to name a few. When a number of components have been identified, a facilitator helps participants see that these can be grouped into four broad areas that represent the four domains of the tool: health, psychosocial/spiritual, human rights and legal, and livelihood security.

How has an individual's QoL changed over time?

To assess how an individual's QoL has changed, the tool requires participants to consider the energy levels of their batteries at two or more points in time. This should ideally be done by carrying out the process at different stages in a programme. Alternatively, it can be done as a retrospective process where the

Table 7.1 Components and domain groupings from Maryknoll Sisters, Cambodia

Health	Psychosocial/spiritual	Human rights/legal	Livelihood security
Sufficient access and adherence to HIV treatment	Support and encouragement from family, friends, and community	No discrimination from government officials	Access to jobs
Treatment for opportunistic infections	No discrimination	Right to legal services and police support	Access to start-up capital
Enough food	Sharing (meals and clothes)	Right to participate in community meetings and express ideas	Sufficient salary
Sleep	Spiritual support from Buddhist pagodas or church	Free access and sufficient supply of antiretrovirals	Enough income for rent and children's education
Exercise		Right to travel	Suitable shelter
Good advice from doctors	Beautiful scenery and entertainment to reduce stress	Right of children to attend school	
Good sexual health			

participant considers their QoL at present and then thinks back to how it was at a previous point in time or before joining the programme.

Each battery is divided into levels (1 to 10, representing low to high energy levels) to help measure and record the client's assessment of each domain. Participants use the scale to assign a 'fullness' level to each battery that best represents their QoL at the present point in time. Ideally, participants should be encouraged to think beyond how they are feeling that day; they should consider how they are feeling at that point in their life. If the process is being carried out retrospectively, participants can then assign a 'fullness' level to a second set of batteries to represent their QoL at a previous point in time. This could be a set period at an earlier point in time (e.g. six months ago or one year ago), or the period of time before they joined the programme.

When assigning energy levels to their batteries, participants should consider the reasons why their QoL is at the selected level. If the batteries are being completed for a second time, or being completed retrospectively, it is important to record reasons for any changes observed in their QoL. These can be recorded by the individual completing the Batteries Tool process, or by the peer supporter or staff member facilitating the process. Participants also reflect on who is responsible for the change, allowing a certain degree of attribution of the change to the programme, client, or another stakeholder.

After participants have assigned scores and reasons for their energy levels and recorded any changes, it is important to get them to think about the things either they, or the programme, can do under the four domains to further improve their QoL. This is a vital component of the process – one that is both encouraging and motivating.

The tool enables the capture of both quantitative scores and qualitative information. The 10-point analogue scale is not prescribed (so what a score looks like is not defined); instead, it is reflective of what an individual feels. The scoring reflects an individual's perception of how they gauge their QoL at one point in time in relation to each of the four domains, which can then be compared with a score they give at a later point in time. The focus is on the difference in scores *over time*, and the difference in scoring levels *between* the domains.

Administering the Batteries Tool

Although the tool is relatively simple, facilitation is usually required. The type and degree of facilitation can vary according to the context in which the tool is being used. The tool can be administered either in a group workshop setting or on a one-to-one basis with individuals as they engage with a programme (e.g. during a clinic or home visit). There are advantages and disadvantages to both.

Where support is needed for individuals to carry out the process, this would ideally be provided by peers trained in the methodology. Where this is not an option, support can be given by programme staff or volunteers.

The process may also include a focus-group sharing option, depending on individual preferences, programme capacity, and cultural contexts. This is important, especially in the initial stages of using the tool, to get a group concept of the components that make up a full and happy life.

Using the Batteries Tool

As discussed before, the Batteries Tool gathers both individual and community reflections on: what people need to have a good and happy life; any changes that occur in this over time; and the reasons for this change, i.e. whether it can be attributed to the programme intervention or external factors beyond the control of the programme, such as the death of a family member.

Box 7.3 Tips for using the Batteries Tool

Once introduced to the idea of energy levels in batteries as a means of expressing the level of contentment in each domain, it is good to get participants to consider what a 'full' battery would look like and what an 'empty' battery would look like in terms of the components they considered.

When assigning energy levels to their batteries, it is important that participants consider their own situation and not that of their family members, partners, or a person whom they care for: although these things may influence their own QoL, this is a personal reflection.

Using the tool on a one-to-one basis can reduce any additional work that would need to be carried out to set up a workshop, and it can save both programme client and staff time. However, you risk losing the ideas and sharing components of the process, which are really important.

If programme staff are facilitating the process, the potential influence of this relationship on the information provided by the programme client needs to be considered.

Box 7.4 Lessons learned

- The four domains identified for the HIV Batteries Tool worked across contexts and countries. They represent the four areas of CAFOD's holistic response to HIV-related care, support, and mitigation and, in turn, the areas that need to be addressed to support an improvement in QoL.
- Through extensive piloting in over 12 countries, experience has shown that the components that come up for people living with and affected by HIV have generally clustered around the four domains outlined in the tool. Although they may vary slightly, they are generally similar. There are no right or wrong answers for which components fit into which domains, and there will always be overlap.
- The concept of batteries and their energy levels seems to translate into different contexts. For example, in Kenya the concept is introduced by getting participants to look at their mobile phones and talking about the charge on their phone battery. In Ethiopia, the concept is introduced through talking about rechargeable batteries used in lamps.

Both the process of using the Batteries Tool and the information that it gathers have been shown to be useful and reflective at different stages of the process and for different stakeholders.

Individuals and communities

By personally reflecting on what it means to have a good and happy life, and considering where they have been and what they have achieved, participants who use the tool have found it to be empowering and motivating. It is a good way of reflecting on what people want to achieve or can do to further improve their QoL. The process supports individuals to realize their rights and what they can and should receive in terms of support. By developing individual action plans, goals can be set, and how they will be achieved can be identified. This will mean thinking through whether the goals can be supported by the organization or whether they are individual goals that can be achieved without support. Where participants have regrouped to share their batteries and reflections, it has been a positive and affirming process for those involved. The process has been likened to a group counselling session where individuals have felt less isolated because others are going through similar experiences.

Programme monitoring and development

The information gathered from individual batteries can improve service provision, particularly the case management of individuals. For example, reviewing the individual batteries enables the service provider to understand the challenges an individual faces and to work with them both to develop and to implement action plans. The process engages clients in programme design by supporting structured reflection on how the programme and other factors have impacted on their lives and on what needs to be done to support them, making the programme more relevant and receptive to their needs.

Although the aggregation of data must be done with caution, it can be useful for looking at trends relating to where the programme is having an impact on the lives of those it supports. Aggregation of the data and identifying trends can steer the response of the programme by identifying where programme clients are generally moving up (or down) in their batteries' energy levels. Through the identification of trends, programme strategies can be developed and broader issues arising across programmes can be identified. For example, CAFOD and a number of partners have taken forward the issue of linking HIV programmes to livelihood security work – an area repeatedly identified through the Batteries Tool as one that needs to be addressed if the QoL of programme clients is going to continue to improve.

At CAFOD, the Batteries Tool has been used predominantly in HIV care and support programmes to assess the changes in the QoL of programme clients living with and affected by HIV. It has also been used to support the evaluation of programmes concerned with gender-based violence, integrated community development programmes with indigenous communities, and child-focused programmes; in these cases, the domains were variable and not predefined, as they have been for HIV programming. The tool has also been adapted to look at other areas of impact related to QoL, including livelihood assets and resilience.

Case study: Brothers of Good Works Counselling and Social Services Centre, Addis Ababa, Ethiopia[1]

Brothers of Good Works Counselling and Social Services Centre (BGW CSSC) first used the Batteries Tool in 2011. Staff selected 40 clients who had recently joined the programme and followed them over the next two years, using the Batteries Tool each year (a total of three times, including the baseline) to assess changes in their QoL.

Initially, BGW CSSC brought programme clients together to introduce them to the tool and to the concept of QoL, and to go through the process of generating ideas on what it meant to them to have a good and happy life. Through this, the components for the four domains that were relevant in this particular context and to these programme clients were elicited, and the group formed a common understanding of these and where they sat within the four domains.

Staff decided to use the tool on a one-to-one basis, with staff members supporting individual programme clients to complete their batteries. They felt that respondents would be much more open in this situation and find it easier than completing their batteries on their own or in a group setting.

BGW CSSC also felt that completing the batteries template on paper would not translate well for the participants, so they decided to use a system of pouring coloured water into glasses, with the glasses representing the batteries and the coloured water the energy levels. The client pours water into the glass to show the level of contentment in each domain. The level of the coloured water is then measured using a purpose-made paper ruler, which is the same height as the glass, with 10 points representing the scale. This adjustment made the tool more accessible, understandable, and visual for clients.

The Batteries Tool data

A wealth of information was gathered using the tool, helping programme staff improve their support to individual clients, address gaps in the programme, and report to donors on these changes in relation to their programme response across the four domains.

At the end of two years, data for 34 participants was available. Of these, 27 clients were female. No one reported improvement across all four domains, but 35 per cent (n=12) had either improved or stayed the same over the four domains. On average, the psychosocial/spiritual and livelihood security domains saw the greatest improvement by the end of the two years. The table below shows the numbers of participants that showed either improvement or no change, or a decrease in their domain scores from the baseline to the third assessment with the tool.

Health domain. Of 34 participants, 47 per cent (n=16) showed improvement from the baseline. This was the domain with the lowest number of participants showing overall improvement and also the greatest number of decreases in score by the end of the second year. At the baseline, participants cited receiving HIV treatment as a positive reason for their scores, but a lack of nutritional support or a balanced diet as reasons that their scores could not be higher. On average, scores increased by one point at the end of the first year but then remained the same at the end of the second year.

Over the two years, specific medical conditions were cited as the main obstacle for not moving up in the health domain. Staff noted that clients were informing them that overall their health was improving due to treatment adherence and seeking medical support, but if they did not feel well at the time they were completing their batteries (even if the condition was temporary or minor), this negatively influenced their health score.

Challenges relating to economic support to cover health costs were mentioned throughout the three rounds of reporting, although the frequency with which they were mentioned diminished slightly by the final year. Individual action plans focused on getting financial and food support. This

Table 7.2 BGW CSSC participants (n=34) showing changes in the Batteries Tool scores over two years (three rounds of reporting)

	Health	Psychosocial	Social rights[2]	Livelihood security
Improved	16	17	5	22
Decreased	11	7	8	6
No change	7	10	21	6

financial support was often spoken about as vital to cover specific healthcare costs. The need for nutritional support was mentioned less as a challenge at the end of years one and two, which seemed to indicate that these needs had been addressed adequately by the programme.

Psychosocial/spiritual domain. Low scores at the baseline were linked with worries about health and economic challenges. The positive reasons for a score were mostly attributed to counselling, which at BGW CSSC addresses issues of family involvement and disclosure. While about half of the respondents mentioned family or community support as a *positive*, an almost equal number mentioned this as a *negative* and as a challenge during the baseline assessment.

Action plans in the first year, as with the health domain, highlighted the need to engage in income-generating activities (IGAs) and the need for some kind of financial support. Respondents also talked about improving health-seeking behaviour. The action plans in the first year also mentioned, although to a lesser extent, the need to continue going to counselling and to work on relationships.

In subsequent years, respondents increasingly mentioned disclosure to and support from friends, family, and neighbours as a reason for their increased score. At the end of the second year, in addition to these reasons, participation in group activities, specifically coffee ceremonies, good relationships and friends, acceptance of their status, and a decrease in the stigma faced from the community were all cited as positive changes and reasons for an increase in scores. Action plans focused mainly on individual actions such as participants' communication with neighbours, going to religious places, and socializing with friends, family, and neighbours.

Social rights domain. Non-Ethiopian non-governmental organizations are not permitted to work on human rights in Ethiopia; for this reason, BGW CSSC renamed this domain 'social rights'. The challenges in discussing these issues were reflected in the notes and scores given in this domain of the Batteries Tool. Much of the discussion was on social relationships and less on more specific issues such as housing or discrimination from employers or those in authority.

Most of the challenges mentioned at the baseline were around discrimination by the community and stigmatizing words from those who did not know how HIV was transmitted. There were, however, a surprising number of positive responses and a significant number scoring themselves 10 on their social rights at the baseline, citing that they had good relationships with their neighbours and their community – very much a focus on social relationships. Action plans for the baseline year mentioned addressing a lack of awareness of HIV in the community and tackling stigma and discrimination; the plans also mentioned building good social relationships.

There were very few negative issues mentioned in the following two years. A few mentioned that things had not changed, but many claimed that there was now no discrimination and that they had counselling and family support. As with the baseline, building social relationships and participating in social activities were mentioned as actions during the second two years. One individual mentioned that they wanted to share their experience with others, and other clients said that they wanted to engage in raising community awareness.

Programme staff saw that this domain was mainly translated in terms of clients' participation in the community, and to a lesser extent in terms of housing issues. One client said that she had to do an HIV test before being employed (which is illegal), but the client did not consider this as an act of discrimination. Staff found discussions in this domain challenging, and managers realized that both clients and staff were not adequately recognizing or addressing aspects of human or social rights.

This domain, in the Ethiopian context, is now better understood by the BGW CSSC staff and programme clients and, as a result, is better addressed. It is acknowledged that reasons for positive scores, such as participation in the community, are a sign of decreasing stigma and discrimination.

Livelihood security domain. Economic challenges were mentioned repeatedly throughout discussions on the other three domains. Scores in the livelihood security domain reflect this and the prominence of these challenges in people's lives – on average, they were much lower than those in the other domains. In 2011, nearly all respondents mentioned food support or the lack of money for food as a reason why they gave relatively low scores in the livelihood security domain. Challenges mentioned included no job or income, and many mentioned high inflation and the economic crisis as an issue. A few mentioned a lack of training and health issues as challenges to their livelihood security domain.

Over the following two years, a number of respondents mentioned starting a new job and then wanting a better job or wanting their family members to engage in IGAs. Action plans continued to highlight the need for business and skills training and engagement in IGAs; however, the involvement of clients in IGAs beyond small businesses is limited due to low levels of education and literacy. By the end of the second year, nearly all respondents mentioned being engaged in IGAs, reflecting the structure of the programme, which supports clients to become economically independent.

Experience of the programme

BGW now uses the Batteries Tool on a one-to-one basis with clients enrolled on all their CSSC programmes. This gives staff the opportunity to explore clients' responses and engage them in meaningful conversation around the support that they need. The Batteries Tool is used directly after a client's admission into the programme, at the end of the first year, and then when they are discharged. Staff working with these clients use the information from the tool to develop and evaluate individual empowerment plans and inform decisions on when clients are ready to complete the programme.

Although data from the tool is not complicated to compile or difficult to analyse, it does take time. Staff at BGW CSSC are committed to analysing the data collected from all clients each year from the various departments of the centre in order to review the individual empowerment programme, inform overall evaluations, and make modifications to the programme where necessary.

One of the challenges in using the tool is the variation in facilitation of the process. BGW CSSC hopes to address this by supervising data collection more closely to improve the quality of the data. BGW has also found that there are challenges in using the tool with clients who are visually impaired. Staff have adjusted the tool for use by care givers and parents of children with disabilities, as well as for orphans and vulnerable children.

The information gathered from the Batteries Tool has highlighted the fact that a holistic response to the care and support of people living with HIV is needed to improve the quality of their lives. Staff saw how the domains were interrelated, and participants often spoke about different domains at the same time or ended up repeating themselves when discussing each domain. This demonstrated how one domain can influence another. This was especially the case with livelihood security issues, which had an impact in all four domains. For example, health cannot be addressed on its own without livelihood security and psychosocial support. BGW has to address these different aspects to support clients to change and improve their lives.

The tool has helped BGW CSSC look at how its interventions have addressed issues and challenges in different areas of its clients' lives. Using the tool has been encouraging for staff, as it has highlighted the contribution of their work to these positive changes. It has enabled staff to support clients to address issues that may not otherwise have been raised.

Using the tool has also been beneficial for clients. It supports them in recognizing that they can take care of developing their own empowerment and can measure changes for themselves. It has also helped clients prepare for the end of their time with the programme, draw lessons from their experience in the programme, and build confidence to seek further improvements in their own lives.

Strengths and limitations

The Batteries Tool goes beyond looking at HIV as simply a health issue and supports programmes to look at the wider picture in terms of QoL. The four domains identified by the Batteries Tool offer a comprehensive framework in which to do this.

The Batteries Tool has various benefits that have been identified at different stages and by different actors throughout the process. Through use of the tool, clients have reported a greater sense of involvement in programme development and a sense of ownership. Just the process of using the tool has been reported by both clients and programme staff as being empowering. The tool facilitates detailed conversations between programme staff and clients, and also between clients, providing a space for them to discuss what is important in their lives. Programme staff get valuable insights into both the individual challenges of clients – challenges that may not have been identified previously – and wider programme impacts and challenges that need to be addressed. Clients reported increased awareness of their own role in improving their QoL.

The tool is simple to use and does not require excessive time, resources, or skills in data collection and analysis. The tool was developed by communities and CAFOD partners working on HIV, and aims to be a client-led process. It is usable by those with low levels of literacy and is easily translatable across languages without too much concern about direct translation of specific questions.

There are also limitations and challenges to the framework despite the tool being relatively simple to use. It requires relatively strong facilitation skills to draw out responses and reasons for changes in the scores. These are useful for both the individual and the programme, and go beyond simply confirming that clients are engaged in certain programme activities. For example, a client simply reporting that their health has improved because they are now on treatment is something that would already be recognized by the programme. Asking the client to talk in more detail about any challenges they have with treatment and how this affects their health or emotional wellbeing would be more useful and would help the programme make appropriate adjustments in the support provided. As with all programme monitoring, it is a challenge to ensure that the information coming out of the tool is used to support the continued improvement in QoL of programme clients and the programme development required to do this.

As the components for each domain are not prescribed, there is room for crossover between the domains, and there can be varying and subjective interpretations of each domain. The extent to which the Batteries Tool yields consistent measurements is, hence, uncertain. This lack of reliability makes aggregation of the data, looking at trends, and drawing conclusions tenuous. The tool has therefore not been statistically validated.

Programme staff have found it challenging to address issues raised by respondents that are beyond the control of the programme. It may be difficult to manage the expectations of clients in terms of what the programme can support and provide. Good facilitation is required to ensure that the specific impact of the programme and the other factors are separated out.

In monitoring changes over time, the limits of using a 10-point scale have been a challenge. As factors such as health improve, aspirations for what can be achieved in terms of health and other aspects of wellbeing may also increase. Respondents may have changing perceptions of what it means to have a good and happy life. Many of the clients who have used the tool see dramatic changes in their health when they begin treatment, and this is reflected in a significant increase in scores in their heath domain. With the initial marked improvement, particularly in the health domain, there is less room to move up the scale in the future, making the quantitative recording of changes in QoL different over time.

Conclusion

CAFOD and CAFOD's partners have learned a significant amount from using the Batteries Tool in terms of the process, their programmes, and the impact that their support is having on the lives of people living with and affected by HIV. The tool has supported partners to strengthen their programme responses and for individuals engaged in the programmes to realize how they can better support themselves. There is still work that can be done on strengthening the process, such as addressing how the data can be better used to inform programme development, but overall the experience of using the tool has been positive, effective, and empowering for those whom it ultimately seeks to support in an improvement in their QoL.

Endnotes

1. This section was written by Christina Maasdam and Solomon Girma.
2. See the paragraph on 'Social rights' for an explanation of why this domain was changed from 'Human rights and legal'.

Harriet S. Jones is the HIV Monitoring, Evaluation, and Learning Coordinator for the Catholic Agency for Overseas Development (CAFOD). She has worked in the HIV sector since 2007. Much of her work focuses on the use of participatory approaches for people living with and affected by HIV to assess changes in their quality of life, and tools to monitor and drive comprehensive programme responses to HIV. Harriet previously worked in the HIV unit at Christian Aid and for the Australasian Society for HIV Medicine. She has a master's degree in international public health from the University of Sydney.

CHAPTER 8

Trócaire: measuring change, person wellbeing, and programme impact using the Wheel

Fiona O'Reilly

The Wheel is a tool designed to measure programme impact on the lives of people living with HIV in community settings in Kenya. It examines six key areas of life: wellbeing, health, prevention, income, belonging, and coping. The tool uses a participatory approach to generate data on the basis of a structured conversation between a project worker and a client. This is guided by questions about knowledge and behaviours related to the key areas. The client moves a counter along the spokes of a wheel image. Summary scores are arrived at for each area and low scores identify areas that need to be worked on to improve health and wellbeing. The individual scores can be aggregated and analysed to inform programme direction and meet the reporting requirements of donors.

Keywords: measurement tool, quality of life, people living with HIV, participatory monitoring, measuring health and wellbeing

Introduction

In a climate of funding crisis, nationally and globally, many non-governmental organizations (NGOs) find that they have to justify the good work they do, previously rarely questioned, in ways that are becoming less meaningful to their client base and programmes. Conversations with NGO colleagues demonstrate their frustration as funders generally want to see the impact of programmes in narrowly defined quantitative terms. Programme officers on the ground, in some of the poorest countries in the world, often have a very good sense of the difference that specific interventions are making. However, translating this into percentage point differences in the lives of people living with HIV as a result of programme interventions, for example, presents a significant challenge.

http://dx.doi.org/10.3362/9781780448411.008

Box 8.1 Trócaire

Trócaire is the overseas development agency of the Catholic Church in Ireland. Established in 1973, today Trócaire works in 20 countries on both long-term development programmes and emergency responses. Trócaire works in partnership with local civil society organizations to tackle social injustices related to sustainable livelihoods, gender equality, HIV, human rights, and emergency relief.

Trócaire envisages a just and peaceful world, where people's dignity is ensured and rights are respected; where basic needs are met and resources are shared equitably; where people have control over their own lives; and where those in power act for the common good.

This emphasis on quantifying programme impact and value for money is not confined to the development sector; it is also influencing programme reporting, albeit to a lesser degree, in the voluntary sector in the UK and Ireland. This drive is not coming solely from funding organizations – practitioners working in the sector are themselves becoming fatigued and frustrated that the social injustices they seek to address, such as homelessness and addiction, are slow to show 'impact' according to hard measurements of change (e.g. numbers of people housed or abstinent from drugs or alcohol). There is a drive, therefore, to demonstrate the consequences of the interventions aimed at improving the lives of the poor and marginalized in a meaningful and real way (MacKeith et al., 2008).[1]

Trócaire, like many other development NGOs, had been grappling with the need to show change as a result of programmes and consequently moved to a results-based management (RBM) model. This required coming up with SMART[2] indicators of programme outcomes that could reliably reflect the changes being delivered as a result of the programme. While this sounds feasible, the reality is that measuring and presenting changes in people's lives in a way that can speak to local programme partners and participants and also meet the needs of administrators and donors is not a simple task.

It is against this backdrop that the Wheel tool was developed to measure change in health and wellbeing among people living with HIV.

The purpose of the Wheel

The Wheel was developed to assess the impact of Trócaire's HIV programme in Kenya, which focuses on improving the quality of life of 7,300 adults and children infected and affected by HIV who are living in slum areas of Nairobi and Nakuru. This involves increasing access to, and the uptake of, HIV services as well as ensuring that those infected and affected by HIV are provided with the care and support they need (physical, psychosocial, and socio-economic) to live meaningful lives.

Through discussion with Trócaire programme staff and by reviewing the results framework for the programme, the following six key areas were

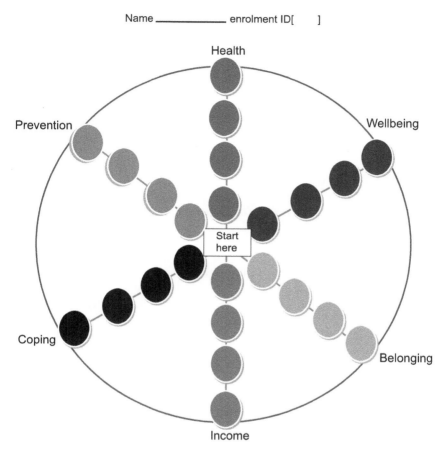

Name _____ enrolment ID[   ]

Figure 8.1 Trócaire's Wheel: assessing improvement in quality of life

identified as being important to people's quality of life: health; lifestyle to promote wellbeing; social belonging; income generation; coping emotionally and mentally; and knowledge and practice around prevention. The assumption is that if people are doing well in each of these six areas, they are more likely to enjoy good health and quality of life. If a person's level of wellbeing could be captured on introduction to the programme, and after the person had been with the programme for some time, then change could potentially be measured. A crude prototype of the Wheel, developed and tested in Mozambique, provided encouraging results. Users reported that the tool was easy and enjoyable to use and it provided a sense of people's wellbeing that could be translated into quantitative data. It was also capable of identifying needs and therefore very useful for programme planning.

Wheel spokes

Each spoke on the Wheel represents one of the six areas identified as being important for a good quality of life. Each spoke has four points or subcategories of information that are scored positively (✓) or negatively (✗) based on information provided by the person living with HIV. For each spoke or 'life area', there is a potential top score of 4 (see Figure 8.1). If a person achieves a score of 4, it means that they are doing very well in that area of their life; if they have a score of 1 or 2, it means they are not doing well and have outstanding needs in that area.

Health. This assesses whether the person is able to look after his or her health. Someone will score highly if they are attending appointments regularly, adhering to treatment, accessing treatment for opportunistic infections, and drinking safe water.

Wellbeing. This spoke gives an indication of whether the person has adopted a healthy lifestyle to promote wellbeing. Scores are based on avoidance of cigarettes and alcohol, use of mosquito nets, taking rest and exercise, having a healthy diet and maintaining one's weight, and feeling healthy.

Belonging. With support, people who are HIV positive can live positively and productively as part of a family and community. The person will score highly in this section if they belong to a peer group, enjoy supportive relationships, and feel that they belong positively and productively within their community.

Coping. This assesses whether the person is supported to cope emotionally and mentally. This is scored on having psychological support at home, attending counselling, and not experiencing depression or feelings of guilt and self-stigma.

Income. This section assesses the person's capacity to generate income and cope economically. Capacity to generate income is scored on involvement in an income-generating activity, or other employment, attainment of household food security, and avoidance of negative coping strategies.

Prevention. This assesses whether the person knows how to reduce the risk of transmission. It is scored on condom use, the importance of disclosure to sexual partners, and knowledge of how to reduce the risk of mother-to-child transmission.

The spokes outlined above represent six areas identified by Trócaire's programme participants in Kenya as being important for a good quality of life. The four points along each spoke represent knowledge or behaviours that the programme deems essential to fully achieve a particular status, for example health or belonging. The questions relating to each point were derived from the programme objectives, knowledge on best practice, and Kenyan national guidelines (Ministry of Public Health and Sanitation, 2010). For example, disclosure of HIV status to sexual partners is advised by national guidelines and is something the programme supports. Therefore, this provides a point on the 'prevention' spoke. Each point on the spoke should constitute an important contribution to the overall area; it should, however, also be an aspect that the programme aims to influence.

It is likely that in another context, where the aim is to support a different target group to achieve different goals, a similar tool could be developed where different spokes or areas of life are identified, and likewise different points along each spoke could be represented. This would need to be tried and tested with the relevant target group.

The scoring system

The aim is to arrive at a point on each spoke of the Wheel that reflects how the person is doing on that area of life. The score (0–4) is arrived at through discussion with the person and is based on self-reporting. It reflects the client's perspective as they are the ones providing the information and, through the process, they gain an understanding of what needs to be achieved in order to get a higher score. As the interviewer (who can be a project worker) is asking the questions, the person moves a counter along the spoke in response to the questions being asked. If the answer is positive, the person moves the counter forward. If it is negative, the counter stays where it is. The interviewer ticks the appropriate circles on the assessment sheets that correspond to each spoke (see Figure 8.2 for an example of one of the six assessment sheets).

Once one spoke has been completed, the counter is placed back at the centre of the Wheel and an X is marked on the point of the spoke in place of the counter. The interviewer then proceeds with the next set of questions relating to the next spoke and the process is repeated. The interview takes the form of a guided discussion and the interviewer is permitted to engage the respondent in informal conversation as long as the relevant information is captured.

At the end of the interview, a pencil line is drawn to join the Xs. In a very positive scenario, where the person receives top scores on each spoke, a full circle will be drawn. When they enrol on a project, the individual's 'circle' may be small or misshapen, but at the end it may be large and full. The shape and size of the circle lets project workers know which areas the person needs most help and support with.

To use the health spoke as an example, the programme aims to support people living with HIV to be as healthy as possible. Four desirable outcomes that the programme can influence are: 1) regular clinic attendance; 2) good medication adherence; 3) reduced risk of opportunistic infection; 4) drinking clean water. Through guided discussions with clients, the community health

Name/ unique identifier _____

Health

This is about how well the person is able to look after him-or herself. It is about being able to manage medication and being able to prepare healthy meals. If someone does not have access to medication or adequate food to prepare healthy meals he or she will not be able to look after themselves properly and so may not be able to score highly in this section.

✓ Move ❶ place on wheel

X Do not move on wheel

a) Do you attend a health centre/clinic?

YES   NO

Is the following true ?   Is the following true?

| You have not missed an appointment in the last 3 months | You have only recently (last month) tested positive and intend not to miss appointment |

Tick if yes

b) **Were you commenced on medication (ART/prophylaxis)?**

YES   NO

Is the following true ?   Is the following true?

| You never or very rarely miss any medication | You have only recently (last month) been diagnosed and intend to have good adherence |

Tick if yes

c) Have you had an opportunistic infection in the last 3 months?

YES   NO

Is the following true ?   Is the following true?

| Was treated for the infection | Knows the importance of treatment and can give examples of opportunistic infections (malaria, diarrhoea, TB, respiratory tract infection) |

Tick if yes

d) Is the water you drink safe?

| On inspection or further questioning the drinking water is safe |

Tick if yes

Figure 8.2 Assessment sheet for health

worker (CHW) or project worker finds out if these outcomes are being achieved. If two of the desired outcomes are achieved, a score of two will be achieved on the health spoke. The tool prompts discussion and the checking of these indicators, and also allows for the capturing of this information in a numerical way. This is useful in meeting reporting requirements. Importantly, however, the discussion is relevant for the client and the worker, independent of reporting needs.

Case studies: Joseph and Judith[3]

These case studies are based on interviews with two programme participants – Joseph and Judith – and a review of their Wheel assessment forms and scores. Both participants completed two Wheels.

Joseph Mutisya is a 45-year-old married man with six children. Joseph lives with his family in Makuru, Nairobi. He works to provide for his family as a casual labourer and by selling second-hand clothes. Joseph first visited Mater Hospital in 2007. He was very sick and had an abscess on his face. He had been tested for HIV elsewhere and referred to Mater when the result was positive.

Joseph first completed the Wheel with a Mater CHW in August 2012. He felt comfortable answering the questions. He described his first Wheel result as a zigzag – some spokes were at a low level, and some were a little bit higher. He said he scored worst in the health, wellbeing, and income areas (see Figure 8.3).

The first time he did the Wheel, Joseph suffered from self-stigmatization and did not want to tell others he had tested positive. His adherence to treatment suffered because he did not want other people to know that he was taking medication and therefore he kept it hidden. He did not have anyone to support him to take his medicine routinely.

A review of the health spoke of his Wheel shows that he received a negative score in relation to question 'b' on adherence (Figure 8.2). On the wellbeing spoke, he received two negative scores: the first because he did not use a mosquito net, and the second because he had not maintained a stable weight. On the income spoke, he received two negative scores because of food insecurity. He scored well on the belonging and coping spokes as he had been a programme member for some time and was accessing support groups. The comment box at the end of the Wheel assessment form noted that Joseph required help with adherence and income generation.

Disclosure for Joseph has meant that he can access support. The support received from the Mater included training to improve treatment adherence, funds to improve his business, and training to increase his business skills, as well as support and advice through home visits. Mater also facilitated the establishment of the 'Hope and Joy' support group that Joseph joined. He is now a founder member of 'Mater Men' – a male champions group for men living with HIV.

Disclosure has further meant that Joseph's family support him, particularly with adherence. Joseph's treatment buddy is his wife, who also tested positive for HIV. He is her treatment buddy. His two older children are aware of their parents' status, and they, too, support their adherence. His mother also supports him. He says his behaviour has also changed: 'I'm not taking beer; I changed my behaviour. I have one partner.' Now he says

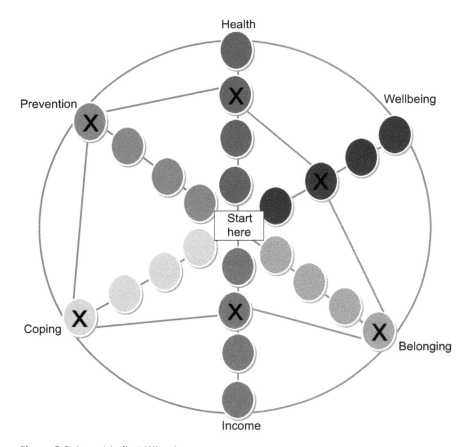

Figure 8.3 Joseph's first Wheel

that he is at about 90 per cent on most spokes: 'I can say I'm improving,' he says. 'When I see that my Wheel goes round, I can encourage others to do better.' He is now supporting others in his community to seek testing and support.

On review of Joseph's second Wheel assessment form, carried out six months after the initial Wheel, we can see that his health spoke improved because of better adherence (Figure 8.4): he began using the recommended mosquito net to reduce the risk of getting malaria and his weight stabilized. His income spoke improved by 1 point; however, he still went without food some days in the previous month and, therefore, could not reach the optimum score for this spoke.

Judith Awino is a 30-year-old married woman with HIV. She has five children and lives in Makuru, Nairobi. Her husband, who is also living with

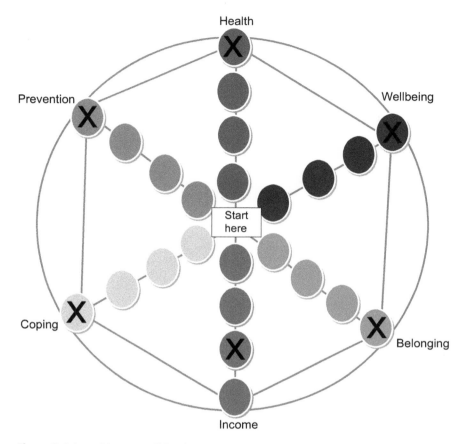

Figure 8.4 Joseph's repeat Wheel

HIV, works as a watchman. Judith first came to Mater for voluntary counselling and testing (VCT) in 2005 after her husband had disclosed his positive status. He accompanied her as she went to get tested. Once she tested positive, Judith began to access support from Mater.

As the Wheel was not developed when she first came to Mater, she does not have one to show for that time, but she says it would not have been good. She first completed the Wheel in November 2012. At this time she says her treatment was going fine and she was generating some income through baking cakes and selling smoked fish. A review of Judith's Wheel shows that she was doing well on the health, prevention, and belonging spokes, which was to be expected as she was an active participant in the programme. However, she did not receive the top score on the wellbeing spoke as she was not able to maintain a stable weight. The lower score on the income spoke was due to

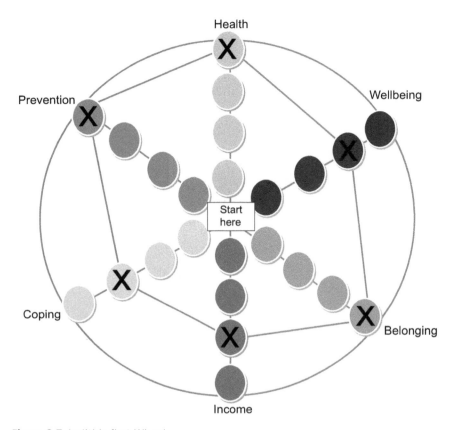

Figure 8.5 Judith's first Wheel

the fact that she had gone without food for a day or more in the preceding month. The coping spoke was also lower because she had suffered bouts of depression. However, it is not clear whether this was in the recent past or the distant past.

Judith received support for her business through Mater. This, she says, enabled her children to eat well and go to school. She accessed her medication through Mater and was visited by the Mater CHW, who she finds very supportive.

Her mother, father, husband, and oldest daughter (13 years) all know her status. 'I tell people my status because they can help me,' she explains. Judith referred a friend to Mater for VCT, explaining that, 'If you know your status, you should tell somebody, then that person can go for VCT.' Judith's treatment buddy is her husband and she attends the Chanuka support group.

Judith has maintained good scores on the spokes of her Wheel, with an improvement recorded against the wellbeing spoke as a result of her now

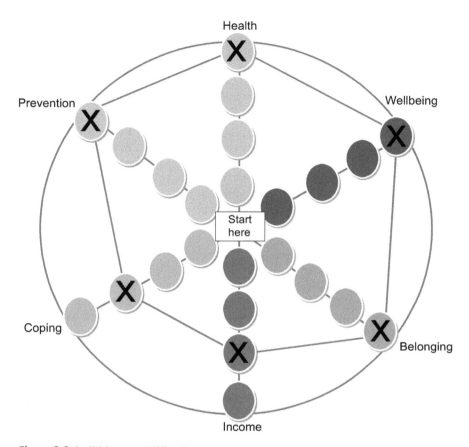

Figure 8.6 Judith's repeat Wheel

maintaining a stable weight (Figure 8.6). Her knowledge and practice of prevention is good, her health is good, and her sense of belonging remains good. She reflects on how far she has come since she first tested positive. 'I don't have any problem in my life now,' she says. The thing she most wants to improve on her Wheel is the income spoke – she would like her business to grow.

Programme monitoring and evaluation

Both Joseph's and Judith's Wheels show some improvement. The visual image helped identify clearly which areas they needed to work on and which areas of support were needed from the programme. When a low score is found on a particular spoke, the answers to the questions relating to that spoke are reviewed to establish what must be done to improve the situation. For example, help with adherence and pointing out the importance of using a mosquito net contributed to an improvement in Joseph's health score. Judith's score on the coping spoke may have been higher if the question asking about experience of depression had been defined to a limited time period or phrased in the present tense, i.e. 'Do you experience periods of depression?' rather than 'Have you had periods of depression?' This is important for tools that aim to capture change. Judith will always have a history of depression, but will not always be depressed. Therefore it is important to ask the question in such a way that her current status rather than her history is reflected in the answer.

Because Judith and Joseph had been in the programme for a number of years before the Wheel was introduced, they were already scoring high on some spokes; their knowledge on prevention was good and they were clearly benefiting from the support groups they attended. If the Wheel had been conducted when they were admitted to the programme, the progression and change demonstrated by the tool are likely to have been greater. The aim in working with people living with HIV is to get the Wheel as big as possible (high scores on each spoke) and then to maintain that Wheel as an indication of life quality and general wellbeing. Thus, when optimal wellbeing is achieved, emphasis is placed on maintenance rather than change. Continuous monitoring every three to six months allows for the identification of deterioration, should it occur, and intervention to regain optimum wellbeing status.

Once the Wheel is being used as part of normal monitoring, programme effectiveness can be gauged simply as an aggregation of individuals' changing Wheels. For example, a programme can report the change in participants' Wheels over a given time period in terms of the proportion of participants who moved up on each spoke, the proportion who moved back, and the proportion who remained the same. The programme can report the change between all first Wheels, all second Wheels, all third Wheels, and so on.

Alternatively, average scores on each spoke can be reported. Depending on staffing, the programme can decide how frequently the Wheel should be conducted. As a rule of thumb, it should be completed at least annually, and no fewer than three months should elapse before completing a repeat Wheel. A period of less than three months would be too short to expect change, and waiting any longer than a year would mean that valuable information on clients' progress, or lack of progress, would be lost.

Annex 1 to this chapter provides a detailed description of how data gathered from the Wheel can be used for monitoring and evaluation purposes.

Strengths and limitations of the Wheel

Monitoring at the individual level

In September 2013, Trócaire staff held discussions with programme participants and Mater Hospital staff conducting Wheel interviews. Programme participants reported that they found the Wheel a useful tool to monitor how they are doing and to draw attention to areas that need improvement. The CHWs had received in-depth training on the Wheel before they began to use it with clients, so they did not find it a difficult tool to use. Mater clinic staff found it a useful tool and embraced its use with all participants: 'You use it to find out where the client has a particular problem,' one CHW noted.[4] Some of the questions overlapped on different spokes; however, this did not appear to be a problem as it helped to validate or clarify information in other sections. The length of time it took to administer the Wheel was not an issue once the objective of the tool was explained to clients. It was found that some clients can be shy when it comes to answering questions about sexual relationships, but, again, with proper explanations and assurances of confidentiality this did not pose a major challenge.

Participatory and empowering

The data generated using the Wheel is on the basis of a conversation between project worker and programme participant. The conversation about how the person living with HIV is doing on the six areas of life being assessed is intended to be useful to both the worker and the client, irrespective of the subsequent analysis conducted for programme reporting. Unlike many quantitative-based tools that use closed questioning with limited responses, this tool allows deviation from the question, paraphrasing, probing, and discussion so that the 'correct' answer is a negotiation between the interviewer and the interviewee. The tool is used a bit like a board game with the interviewee moving the counter or pebble along the spokes of the wheel. Once the rules of the game are explained, the person living with HIV, with the help of the project worker, decides where they are on each spoke according to the 'rules'. The qualitative data is immediately turned into scores for easy analysis. On completion of the Wheel, both project worker and participant agree on areas for future focus.

Monitoring at the programme level

As well as having the capacity at an individual level to identify future directions for support, the aggregated analysis of the Wheels identifies what areas the programme should focus on (see Annex 1 of this chapter). It also allows local organizations to meet the reporting requirements of their donors. The quantitative results lend themselves well to the results-based analysis required by an increasing number of donors but without the need for external consultants to fly in, gather data, and fly off again to analyse it. Once trained in its use and its capacity to support monitoring and evaluation, partners can be in full control of measuring the Wheel's effectiveness without external support.

The real benefit of the Wheel is realized if it is conducted on enrolment and over time with the same participants. This allows the programme staff and the new client to identify the areas of support required and to monitor progress on these subsequently.

Limitations

The Wheel has been used in Kenya by Trócaire on a trial basis and by a variety of local NGOs with varied capacity and results. Its usefulness has yet to be formally evaluated but feedback and reflection have highlighted the importance of training in the administration of the tool. To ensure a standardized approach, CHWs need to be trained, supported, and mentored in the use of the tool. Ideally, the same staff member or CHW should administer the repeat Wheel. We have no evaluation as yet of the impact of different interviewers on results.

The Wheel was designed as a tool to help track progress of defined people living with HIV following programme interventions. It requires programme participants to be identifiable and enrolled in the programme and assumes that there will be much contact with the CHWs or project workers; it may not be suitable for very large programmes with a high turnover that do not have this ongoing contact.

Significant change is more likely to be seen if an interview is conducted close to enrolment in the programme. After a length of time in the programme, assuming the participant has benefited fully, the scores on the Wheel will not be expected to change further, and success should be seen as maintenance of what has been achieved. For some clients, significant life changes (for example, the death of someone in the household) had a major impact on their progress, so it is important that this is captured in a comment section.

While CHWs report the successful use of the tool to identify client needs, the aggregated analysis to show programme performance has been more challenging and requires further work. Depending on the specific programme objectives and changes in these over time, some of the questions may need to be altered or replaced.

Finally, the tool itself is paper-based (eight pages), and it can be costly to print. It is advisable to laminate the Wheel and to reuse it. The assessment form can be printed double-sided, in black and white, and ticked in pencil. On repeat use, the ticks can be erased and redone. In this way, one assessment form can be used for multiple assessments.

Future use

The use of the Wheel in Kenya has been championed by one of Trócaire's partner organizations – Mater Hospital. Evaluation and assessment of support needs are now required for its continued use. The use of the Wheel in the Kenya end-line study and comparison with the baseline will allow further reflection on its suitability as a tool for measuring health and wellbeing for people living with HIV in developing countries, and, as such, for measuring results and programme effectiveness.

Annex 1: using the Wheel for monitoring and evaluation

The following is an analysis of the first and subsequent Wheels for 15 of Mater Hospital's participants. The red/dark line represents the optimum scores and the blue/light the actual average scores.

There are numerous ways of analysing the aggregated scores to see how the programme is doing. The diagrams below were derived from averaging each spoke score using Excel and then plotting them on the Wheel. Again, the first Wheels were not done on initial admission to the programme; many participants had been enrolled for some time before the Wheel was completed. This resulted in quite high scores on the first and second Wheels. Nevertheless, improvement can be seen in the coping and income spokes, which indicates that the programme has helped in these areas.

Wheels can be analysed to compare scores by gender or by length of time in the programme. Analysing Wheels on a programme basis can help identify where the programme needs to focus greater attention or modify strategies. For example, if income or food/nutrition security are areas on which people continuously achieve low scores, the programme may need to increase capacity to respond to these factors that are negatively affecting participants' wellbeing.

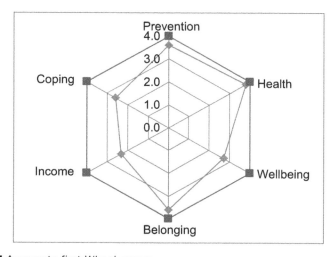

Figure 8.7 Aggregate first Wheel scores

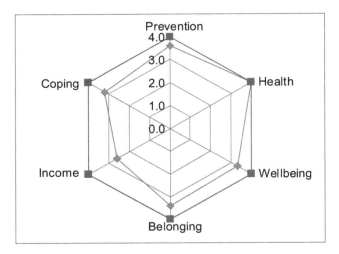

Figure 8.8 Aggregate repeat Wheel scores

Use in the baseline

Trócaire's programme in Kenya had funding for three years and used RBM to identify programme outcomes and indicators. Indicators to show people's health, wellbeing, and quality of life were measured and analysed using the Wheel at the beginning of the programme. The following gives a snapshot of the baseline results that were established using the Wheel data. The Wheel baseline interview assessment was conducted with 116 people living with HIV who were participating in the Trócaire programme.

A systematic random sample was identified, yielding an overall sample of 31 per cent (n=116) of direct programme participants living with HIV. The first section of the Wheel tool collects demographic details. An analysis of this data shows that of the 116 people living with HIV interviewed, 78 per cent were women, 65 per cent were married or cohabitating, and 45 per cent of those who were single had been widowed. Some 42 per cent of households had more than one person living with HIV. All bar one (defaulter) were attending a clinic and 81 per cent were on antiretroviral therapy (ART). Only 32 per cent had reached a post-primary education level, and significantly more men had reached this level than women (p<0.05).

The Wheel in Figure 8.9 shows the average scores on each spoke for the Trócaire Kenya programme. The red line denotes the optimum score, while the blue line joins the average scores to show a less than perfect circle with dips at the income generation and the wellbeing spokes.

Average scores for each spoke are marked on the Wheel and are joined by the blue line. Average scores for health, belonging, and prevention were 3.3, 3.0, and 3.1 respectively. The average score for emotional and psychological coping was 2.8. Average scores for wellbeing and income were somewhat lower at 2.4 each.

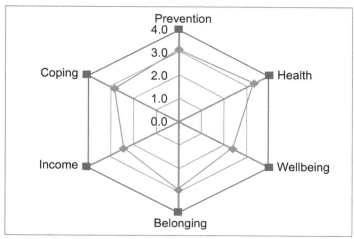

Figure 8.9 Baseline Wheel average scores

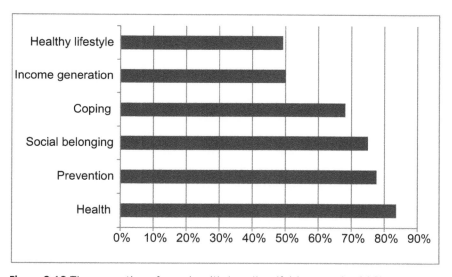

Figure 8.10 The proportion of people with 'good' or 'fair' scores (n=116)

The same data can be analysed to show proportions of people living with HIV according to their scores on each spoke. A score of 2 or less is considered poor, a score of 3 fair, and a score of 4 good.

Most (57 per cent) achieved mid-range scores (>14–19) when the scores on each spoke were totalled. Eighteen per cent scored low (>9–14) and 25 per cent scored high (>19–23). The characteristics of those scoring low and high were examined to reveal that there was a higher proportion of high total scores among support group members (29 per cent) compared with non-support group members (14 per cent) and a lower proportion of low total

Table 8.1 Characteristics of those achieving 'low' and 'high' total scores

	n	High score (>19)	Low score (<14)
Support group member	39	29%	16%
Not in a support group	11	14%	24%
Men	11	36%	8%
Women	38	21%	21%

scores (16 per cent versus 24 per cent). This suggests the benefit of being part of a support group. In a gender comparison of high and low total scores, men were more likely to score high (36 per cent versus 21 per cent) and less likely

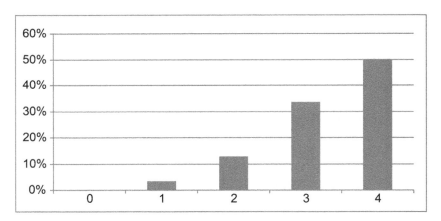

Figure 8.11 Health spoke scores

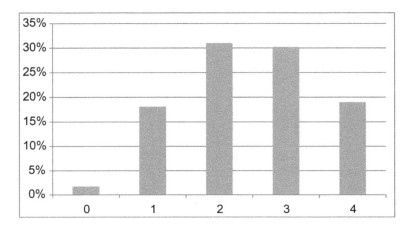

Figure 8.12 Wellbeing spoke scores

to score low (8 per cent versus 21 per cent). However, numbers were small and the significance level was not quite reached (p=0.06).

Individual 'spoke' scores

Health scores are based on attending clinic appointments, good adherence to treatment, awareness and treatment of opportunistic infections, and drinking safe water. The majority (84 per cent) scored 3 or 4 on this. This was the highest-scoring spoke on the wheel.

Wellbeing scores are based on lifestyle factors that contribute to wellbeing – in particular, avoidance of bad habits (cigarettes and alcohol), the practice of good ones (use of mosquito nets and taking rest and exercise), having a healthy diet, and maintaining one's weight. A large proportion (51 per cent) scored poorly on this (≤2).

The income spoke focuses on income generation, employment, and avoidance of negative coping strategies as well as having household food security. Half of the respondents scored poorly on this spoke.

Belonging (social belonging) was scored on group membership, supportive relationships, social activity, and having a productive role in the community. Three-quarters (75 per cent) scored 3 or more on this measure.

Coping (emotionally and mentally) was scored on having psychological support at home, attending counselling, and absence of depression, guilt, and self-stigma. Over two-thirds (68 per cent) scored 3 or more on this spoke; however, a significant minority (32 per cent) scored poorly.

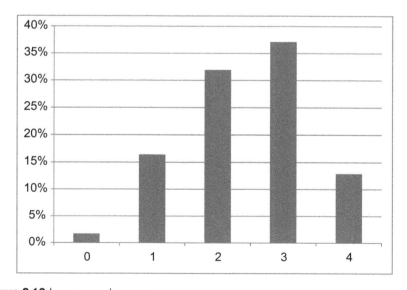

Figure 8.13 Income spoke scores

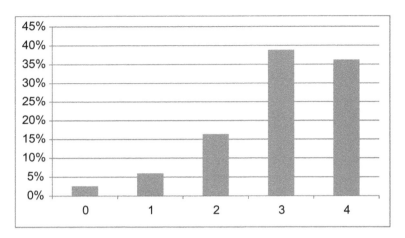

Figure 8.14 Belonging spoke scores

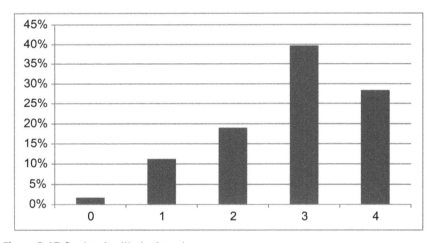

Figure 8.15 Coping (wellbeing) spoke scores

Prevention was scored on individuals' views and practice of disclosure to partners and children, knowledge and practice of safe sex, and knowledge and use of preventative mother-to-child services. This was the second-highest scoring spoke, with 78 per cent scoring 3 or more.

Comment

Most participants (71 per cent) had enrolled in the programme prior to 2012, with 68 per cent having tested positive prior to 2010. With this in mind, one expects a pretty positive picture from the Wheel data for the programme, as most clients are supported in the six life areas that the Wheel assesses. In fact,

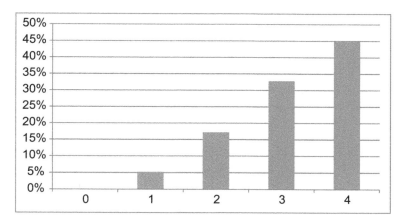

Figure 8.16 Prevention (health) spoke scores

this is what we found. However, there are a number of clear areas identified where more support could be focused, such as clean water, use of mosquito nets, and increase in household food security.

In the comparison analysis, the biggest difference was seen between support and non-support group members. Support group members tended to be worse off economically and in terms of how they viewed their health, suggesting perhaps that those in greater need are more inclined to join groups. Being involved in a support group was associated with positive outcomes – disclosure, positive prevention knowledge and attitudes, and supportive relationships. Being in the programme longer (i.e. enrolling prior to 2012) was associated with coping psychologically and disclosing to partners.

The emphasis of this programme is on maintaining health, wellbeing, and positive living among people living with HIV. The indicators show that this has largely been achieved and suggest that emphasis should be given to expanding the numbers enrolling on the programme and improving Wheel scores, particularly for new participants. The aim for people doing well was to maintain their high scores.

Endnotes

1. Some recent initiatives have aimed to address this need. The Outcome Star, for example, is one such tool developed to capture real and important outcomes in the lives of people affected by homelessness (MacKeith et al., 2008). It can show progression for the person in a number of domains, even if the ultimate aim of being housed has not been attained.
2. SMART means specific, measurable, achievable, relevant, time bound.
3. The names of the participants have not been changed, at their request.
4. Source: discussions with CHWs, Mater Hospital, Nairobi, September 2013.

References

MacKeith, J., Burns, S. and Graham, K. (2008) *The Outcomes Star: Organisation Guide*, 2nd edn, London: Homeless Link and Triangle Consulting.

Ministry of Public Health and Sanitation (2010) *Quick Reference Guide to the HIV Basic Care Package for Community Health Workers and Peer Educators*, Nairobi: Population Services International (PSI/Kenya).

Fiona O'Reilly is a senior research fellow in social inclusion at the University of Limerick, Ireland. She is a social scientist with many years of experience working in overseas development. Her research focuses on health, equity, and justice. Fiona has provided research expertise and technical support to Trócaire on a variety of projects over a number of years.

Acknowledgements

Contributions from Trócaire and Mater Hospital staff to the writing of this chapter are gratefully acknowledged. Thanks are due to the men and women living with HIV in Nairobi who willingly shared their time and experiences. Mater Hospital in Nairobi enthusiastically spearheaded the use of the tool, and thanks are due in particular to Barrack Onyango, Sister Brigid Marnane, and Sister Aine Campell. Daniel Masyuki and the RAOSOK research team as well as Trócaire's partner organizations in Kenya (Love and Hope, St Joseph's and Medical Missionaries of Mary) were involved in testing, refining, and using the tool in the baseline study. The tool was designed by Fiona O'Reilly for Trócaire and evolved out of a desire to ensure that programme monitoring first and foremost serves the needs of beneficiaries. Catherine Khamali, Deirdre Ní Cheallaigh, and Noreen Gumbo of Trócaire co-ordinated the process and provided valuable assistance throughout. For further information please contact Deirdre Ní Cheallaigh at dnicheallaigh@trocaire.ie.

PART THREE

Wellbeing and quality of life in policy and advocacy

Part Three of this book focuses on how a wellbeing approach can be used in policy and for advocacy purposes. As emphasized in the introductory section, prioritizing the wellbeing or quality of life (QoL) of individuals and communities is ultimately a political act. Placing wellbeing or QoL at the centre of policy making means drawing attention to the limitations of using national economic growth (gross domestic product or GDP) as the principal indicator of a country's development – how it does *not* take into consideration either the quality or the equitable distribution of that growth. It also means emphasizing what really matters to people, and advocating for a new set of values that place material sufficiency and environmental sustainability over growth. The contributors to this section (and the previous section) all share the view that in promoting wellbeing and QoL, policy makers must look beyond the individual and their personal happiness and consider how economic, political, and social systems play a significant role in enhancing or undermining people's experience of wellbeing.

In **Chapter 9**, Friends of the Earth draws from its experiences of using a wellbeing approach in its advocacy work to discuss the potential of using the approach in policy making, specifically in promoting sustainable development. The chapter describes a participatory process through which a productive discussion on wellbeing can be facilitated with the aim of influencing policy makers. It suggests the kinds of questions that should be asked, proposes the principles that should govern the discussion, and makes a number of recommendations on how to influence policy making. **Chapter 10** presents Oxfam's Humankind Index – a tool developed to assess the collective prosperity of Scotland. The chapter discusses the political motivation in developing an index that was more holistic and representative of people's priorities than GDP. It describes how the Humankind Index has been used to measure Scotland's prosperity at both the community and national level, and highlights how the index and the information gathered from it have been used to advocate for policies that reflect the needs of deprived communities in particular, and what people felt was important to live well in general. **Chapter 11** focuses on how Wellbeing Wales – a consortium of voluntary organizations – sought to translate Welsh policy that was emphasizing wellbeing into current practice.

It first describes how a Sustainable Wellbeing Framework was used to help transform 'wellbeing' into a tangible concept that could be used for planning, delivering, and assessing services. The chapter then discusses the different processes that were undertaken and the challenges faced in transforming policies on wellbeing into meaningful practice.

CHAPTER 9

The potential for a wellbeing approach in policy making and sustainable development

A. Michael Warhurst

This chapter discusses how a wellbeing approach can be used in policy making. It describes work that is only just beginning, and which has been initiated by Friends of the Earth – the world's largest grassroots environmental network, with over 70 autonomous groups around the world. The work described in this chapter is being developed by Friends of the Earth Europe, in collaboration with Friends of the Earth England, Wales, and Northern Ireland. The chapter focuses more on the potential of a wellbeing approach to create progress towards sustainable development, and discusses some of the central elements a productive discussion on wellbeing should have if it is to promote sustainable development. The chapter also describes in detail a format for conducting a wellbeing discussion, including an agenda, principles for discussion, the role of facilitators, how to deal with conflict, and suggestions for how to incorporate the outcomes of the discussion into policy making.

Keywords: wellbeing, policy making, sustainable development, wellbeing discussions, participatory process

Introduction

Moving society towards sustainability is not straightforward, and requires a wide range of changes. In this process, it is important to develop workable solutions, but it is also vital that people feel ownership of these solutions, and that wide coalitions are formed in favour of these solutions. A wellbeing approach can potentially work both by developing solutions and by ensuring ownership of them.

It is now widely accepted that a focus on growth in gross domestic product (GDP) by itself is not going to create a better society, but there is a lack of agreement on how to resolve this (e.g. BRAINPOOL, 2014). A range of initiatives have been created to examine other options, for example the EU's 'GDP and Beyond' process (European Commission, 2009) and the Stiglitz–

http://dx.doi.org/10.3362/9781780448411.009

Box 9.1 The debate on 'beyond GDP'

Gross domestic product (GDP) is currently the overarching measure of performance for most economies, despite the original developer of the concept, Simon Kuznets, stating in 1934 that 'the welfare of a nation can ...scarcely be inferred from a measurement of national income' (Acting Secretary of Commerce, 1934).

GDP has been critiqued on many fronts in recent years; for example, the European Commission's 'GDP and Beyond' communication and the Stiglitz–Sen–Fitoussi report. The Stiglitz–Sen–Fitoussi report (2009) explicitly calls for a focus on wellbeing within a context of sustainability:

'Another key message, and unifying theme of the report, is that the time is ripe for our measurement system to shift emphasis from measuring economic production to measuring people's well-being. And measures of well-being should be put in a context of sustainability.'

Sen–Fitoussi report (2009). These discussions, however, have a tendency to be quite inaccessible and academic, and are very distant from normal discussions between people and organizations. This distance and abstract process are not helping the political impact of these processes. Hence, they are not significantly impacting on *real* policy making.

In this chapter, I will describe a different approach – a participative discussion (see Box 9.3) that can be undertaken at any level of governance, to discuss a positive vision of the future, and to identify the key (measurable) elements of wellbeing in this future. Such a participative approach aims to ensure relevance to the level of governance, and encourage ownership of, and advocacy for, the outcomes.

Sustainable development

Sustainable development has become a highly contested concept over the years, with other models talking about three pillars of sustainability – environmental, economic, and social. A central focus of the debate has been deciding whether the environment is overarching (as we all depend on our planet for our existence), or whether the economy is the most important thing (as it generates the money and jobs).

In theory, the sustainable development concept is supposed to balance the 'three pillars', but it often just ends up accentuating the differences between them. There is a plethora of sustainable development strategies and processes; however, the conflicts and redefinitions continue.

The 'GDP and Beyond' communication (European Commission, 2009) talks too about wellbeing, including self-reported wellbeing of individuals and communities. It also proposes a 'comprehensive environmental index' – which has so far proved to be unachievable.

However, no alternative to GDP has yet reached the mainstream. Moreover, both of these wellbeing approaches are essentially top-down, in that the indicators of wellbeing are to be defined by experts in statistical offices,

---

Box 9.2 Sustainable development

The concept of **sustainable development** has many definitions, emphasizing different aspects. One of the first is from the World Commission for Environment and Development (Brundtland Commission) in 1987:

'Sustainable development is development that meets the needs of the present without compromising the ability of future generations to meet their own needs. It contains within it two key concepts:

- the concept of **"needs"**, in particular the essential needs of the world's poor, to which overriding priority should be given; and
- the idea of **limitations** imposed by the state of technology and social organization on the environment's ability to meet present and future needs.'

---

researchers, and so on. While such an approach is relevant in some circumstances, a more participative approach may have more power and impact in others.

A participative approach to wellbeing

In order to create a sustainable future, we need to gain broad support for changes in society – changes in our lifestyle, including how and what we consume (e.g. how much meat we have in our diet, how many material possessions we need to own), and how and when we travel (car versus public transport, walking or cycling, train versus plane). Two key elements are required for this:

- a clear idea of what it is that we are trying to achieve;
- broad support for these changes.

It is already well known that it is easier to secure people's commitment to changes if they have been involved in devising them. A participative approach, therefore, should help achieve broader support for change, as more people will feel ownership of the outcomes. In addition, involving more people and groups in the process will increase the information available in the discussion.

Outcomes not policies

A discussion on 'what we are trying to achieve' is quite likely to end up as a focus on *individual policies and plans*. This will be particularly true if professional policy makers are in the room, as they will have a well developed set of policies to promote.

However, I would argue that this discussion actually needs to focus on the *outcomes* we are trying to achieve, not the policies to achieve them. This has the benefit of separating outcomes from policies, as it is generally easier to achieve consensus on outcomes rather than agreeing on policies that are marked by different political beliefs. For this approach to be really effective, it will be necessary for outcomes to be measurable, at least at some point in the near future. Crucially, this process assumes that most people do want to make the world a better place, and that there will ultimately be greater agreement on the outcomes that will help create this 'better place'.

Who should be involved in the discussion?

In order to get a wide range of information and opinions, and to ensure broad buy-in to the outcomes, it is important to ensure that you have a broad group involved in the wellbeing discussion. It is worth thinking about likely issues that could come out of the discussion (e.g. education, health, or poverty) and see if it is possible to get representatives from these groups.

The people who are (and are not) in the room will affect the dynamics of the discussion and its later impacts, as the examples below illustrate.

- If key players are missing from the discussion, this could create a backlash against the outcomes. For example, if traders were omitted from a discussion on the future wellbeing of a town, then they would be less likely to accept the results.
- In larger settings (beyond small communities or organizations), many of the people in the room will end up being some sort of representative of a group of people (stakeholders). This will be unavoidable to an extent, but you could still mix in some individuals, particularly if they come from a group with less effective stakeholder representation, for example people on low incomes or other disadvantaged groups.
- If policy makers are not in the room, it may be easier for the group to come to an agreed set of outcomes that can be presented later to policy makers. Conversely, policy makers may have information that is useful for the discussion, and may be more likely to adopt proposals that they have been involved in creating.
- Elected policy makers and officials have different roles, as do local and national policy makers. It might be appropriate to have officials but not elected policy makers, or local but not national, depending on the circumstances.

If the group organizing the discussion has its own inputs that it wants to make, then it would be wise to do this through a representative within the group, separate from the role of the facilitator. It is important that the facilitator is unbiased, otherwise the group members may feel that they are being led in a certain direction, which will reduce trust in the process (see below).

One option for addressing the representation issue is to have a more iterative process. For example, if excluded groups object to the outcome of the process, then a second round of discussions incorporating these groups could be organized.

A simplified version of the wellbeing discussion could also be created online, for example, allowing people to submit things that they view as important to wellbeing.

What should the question be?

The question that the group is posed will have an impact on the answers received. For example, if people are asked *'What are the important things that would need to happen for your community to have a better quality of life in 10 years?'*, you are likely to get quite locally related answers. In contrast, if you asked *'... for the world to be a better place in 10 years?'*, the answers would most probably have a global dimension to them.

These issues are important because the wellbeing approach has been critiqued for its potential to be individualistic – it can focus on the personal interests of individuals while ignoring issues such as long-term sustainability, global equity, the impacts of people's consumption on the rest of the world, or even local poverty, if these voices are not in the room.

One option is to emphasize the importance of future wellbeing in the question – *'... for you **and** your children – or grandchildren,'* for example. It is also possible to run parallel discussions with different small groups. For example, separate groups could be asked about 'community', 'country', 'Europe' and 'the world'.

A suggested process for the wellbeing discussion

This section provides a suggested process and framework for the wellbeing discussion and its follow-up. The idea is to balance a very participative process with a clear framework that will eventually force prioritization and facilitate effective follow-up into policy making.

Principles of the discussion

- This is a participative process and could happen at any level: between EU stakeholders, at national level, in a school, etc. As mentioned before, it is important to have a diversity of voices in the room.
- This process and the initial follow-up are intended to generate a small number of 'domains' of what constitutes wellbeing (see, for example, the PADHI framework in Chapter 4 and the inner wellbeing model in Chapter 5). This should be followed by a list of components (or outcomes) for each domain (perhaps five or six). Ideally, these outcomes are (or will be) measurable, and an idea of what poor/adequate/good means for each of the domains should be defined clearly.
- The aim is to be able to express the results (top-level and within the domains) in an easy-to-understand visual. A good example of this is how the UK supermarket Sainsbury's implemented the UK Food Standards Agency's food labelling scheme using the traffic light symbol.

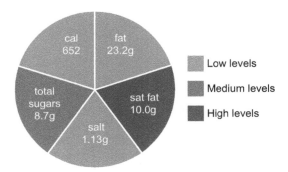

Figure 9.1 Sainsbury's traffic light food label

Role of the facilitators

The role of the facilitators is very important in a wellbeing discussion. They should not be directing the discussion, but they need to be effective at facilitating it. In particular, they need to:

- Allow the discussion to range widely, but without going into excessive depth in specific areas, as this will mean insufficient time for other areas.
- Prompt for thoughts on issues that are likely to be relevant for the group, but which have not been mentioned.
- Drill down to real-world outcomes, not just individual policies – this could include combining different proposed outcomes together: for example, rather than policies of 'providing housing support for vulnerable people' or 'building affordable housing', an outcome could be: 'people live in a home that is warm enough, adequately ventilated, and affordable to heat'.
- Group the outcomes into domains (with the guidance of the group), and also get rid of duplicate outcomes.

Dealing with conflict

There are likely to be conflicts in a group, and the facilitator will need to manage them. In some cases, it may be possible to resolve conflicts by drilling down to the real outcome. For example, shopkeepers may want more parking spaces for potential customers, while residents may want fewer cars parked. The real outcome in this case would probably be that the shops want increased income – parking is just their view of how this income can be achieved.

Once outcomes have been agreed, there is an opportunity to identify and discuss evidence about how to reach those outcomes (for example at later meetings). This is another method that may be able to resolve conflicts, particularly if there is good-quality evidence available.

In some cases it may be necessary to have outcomes that to some extent are in opposition to each other – the reality of policy making is that often you have to balance costs and benefits to different groups. Ideally, this should be avoided wherever possible.

Box 9.3 Wellbeing discussion day

i. **Introduction to the day**
    - Setting the scene: talk about the concept of having a vision of a better future – not just a generic vision, but a specific one. What will the key components be (e.g. health, education, environment, jobs, family, etc.)?
    - This can be preceded by a warm-up session, appropriate to the group (e.g. look at the good and bad points of a neighbourhood, or think about a vision for 2030).

ii. **In groups – components of a better future**
    - Split into groups of four or five. Using Post-it notes, write down all the different components of this future. (Ideally, they should be measurable in some way, although this may not need to be discussed at this stage).

iii. **Plenary – group components into domains**
    - After, say, 30 minutes, come together with Post-its, stick them on a wall, and attempt to group them into domains.
    - Challenge – can we group them to five or six domains?
    - Is there anything missing? This is a chance for other elements to be added on and also to move some components between domains.
    - Sticker prioritization can be used (e.g. each person has six stickers) to resolve differences.
    - Draw a segment pattern and insert five or six domain names, giving draft versions of the top-level domains.

iv. **BREAK**

v. **In groups – what should be in each domain?**
    - Discuss individual domain areas. Start with the Post-its that people already have.

- The number of rounds and groups will depend on the size of the group. It is always good to have more than one discussion on each domain.
- Can we prioritize five or six components for each domain?

vi. **Plenary – agree on the contents for each domain**
    - Go through each domain and the suggestions on which components to fill it with.
    - Try to reach agreement on the contents of each domain (e.g. using sticker prioritization).
    - Explain that we have essentially identified a series of outcomes that we want to see happen.

vii. **Plenary or groups – how do we measure each component? Do we know what the dividing lines are between very good, OK, and bad?**
    - Establish questions for the initial discussions (to be developed further after the meeting, at future meetings, or in discussions).
    - Do we know how to measure each of these outcomes?
    - Do we have any idea about where we would put dividing lines (e.g. red/amber/green)?

viii. **Plenary – agree how the day will be followed up**
    - Can we assign a lead person or group for each domain to continue discussions, with the aim of resolving the outcomes and proposing dividing lines, in consultation with the rest of the group, by a set date?
    - When will we be able to produce the first version of the wellbeing pie charts?

ix. **Initial follow-up**
    - Ensure that lead people resolve the outcomes and proposed dividing lines.

(continued)

- Work with all the participants to see if data is available to give a first idea of the overall outcome.
- Present the outcome to decision makers, media, etc. as appropriate. If there are objections from groups that were not part of the discussion, consider a second round of discussions to include them.

x. **Further follow-up or embedding**
- Compare the agreed domains and outcomes with what the organization

(or government/EU) is currently working towards.
- Develop data sources for the outcomes.
- Work with decision makers to incorporate the proposed domains into the way the organization works, for example by setting targets.
- Identify if evidence is available about policies and approaches that could help achieve the agreed outcomes.

Integration into policy making

As this chapter makes clear, part of the aim of this wellbeing discussion is to influence policy, whether within an organization, a village, a country, or an international level of governance like the European Union.

Effective policy influence will depend on a number of factors:

- relevance to that level of governance – i.e. they will be more interested in outcomes that they can influence;
- wide support among stakeholders;
- easy communicability, including the ability to use the simple 'pie chart' graphics to demonstrate progress;
- clear methods to measure the outcomes;
- a clear rationale for red/amber/green (poor/adequate/good) ratings.

There have been previous efforts to incorporate sustainability into local policy making – notably Local Agenda 21 – which was initially adopted by thousands of communities around the world (United Nations, 2012), although interest has since waned (see Smardon, 2008). This initial success demonstrates that there is a local appetite for this type of discussion.

Conclusions

Taking a wellbeing approach is not going to be a panacea: disputes will remain, sustainability remains difficult, and knowing the outcomes you want does not mean you will achieve them. However, in my view, the wellbeing discussion described in Box 9.3 creates a much more accessible, more participative, more unifying, and more empowering way of discussing and reaching conclusions on complex issues such as sustainable development.

In our initial tests of this approach, Friends of the Earth found that people are energized and enthusiastic at the end of the discussion.

There is evidence that by looking at 'life in the round', a wellbeing conversation is more likely to help people focus more on intrinsic values such as community, family, and green space, and less on extrinsic values such as income and possessions (Blackmore et al., 2013). The wellbeing discussion process, taking place at many different levels in society, could in theory assist in moving society towards a less material, more sustainable future.

We are now taking this wellbeing discussion approach out to our local groups – and to other local communities – around the UK, and to Friends of the Earth groups in other EU countries. We are also working to build a group of civil-society organizations at European level that will use the wellbeing approach to develop a set of outcomes for the EU in the future, which we can then advocate in policy processes.

References

Acting Secretary of Commerce (1934) 'National income, 1929–32: letter from the Acting Secretary of Commerce transmitting in response to Senate resolution no. 220 (72d cong.) a report on national income, 1929–32' <http://fraser.stlouisfed.org/docs/publications/natincome_1934/19340104_nationalinc.pdf> [accessed 29 June 2014].

Blackmore, E., Underhill, R., McQuilkin, J. and Leach, R. (2013) *Common Cause for Nature: Values and Frames in Conservation*, Machynlleth, Wales: Public Interest Research Centre. <http://valuesandframes.org/initiative/nature/> [accessed 22 June 2014].

BRAINPOOL (2014) *Beyond GDP: From Measurement to Politics and Policy*, London: New Economics Foundation and BRAINPOOL. <www.brainpoolproject.eu/wp-content/uploads/2014/03/BRAINPOoL-Final-Conference-Background-Paper-FINAL.pdf> [accessed 22 June 2014].

Brundtland Commission (1987) *Our Common Future*, New York: United Nations World Commission on Environment and Development.

European Commission (2009) *GDP and Beyond: Measuring Progress in a Changing World*, Brussels: Commission of the European Communities. <http://eurlex.europa.eu/LexUriServ/LexUriServ.do?uri=COM:2009:0433:FIN:EN:PDF> [accessed 22 June 2014].

Smardon, R.C. (2008) 'A comparison of Local Agenda 21 implementation in North American, European, and Indian cities', *Management of Environmental Quality: An International Journal* 19 (1): 118–37.

Stiglitz, J.E., Sen, A. and Fitoussi, J.P. (2009) *Report by the Commission on the Measurement of Economic Performance and Social Progress*, Paris: Commission on the Measurement of Economic Performance and Social Progress. <www.stiglitz-sen-fitoussi.fr/documents/rapport_anglais.pdf> [accessed 22 June 2014].

United Nations (2012) *Review of Implementation of Agenda 21 and the Rio Principles*, New York: United Nations Department of Economic and Social Affairs Division for Sustainable Development. <www.uncsd2012.org/content/documents/194Synthesis%20Agenda%2021%20and%20Rio%20principles.pdf> [accessed 22 June 2014].

A. Michael Warhurst has been Executive Director of CHEM Trust (<www.chemtrust.org.uk>) since July 2014. Prior to this he worked for Friends of the Earth in London from 2005, heading up their Economics and Resource Use Programme, and leading Friends of the Earth Europe's (FOEE's) work on resources and consumption. This included developing a programme of work on wellbeing and sustainable development. He has previously worked on waste policy at Friends of the Earth, and also on EU chemicals policy for both Friends of the Earth and World Wildlife Fund's European Policy Office. Michael has an MSc in environmental chemistry from the University of Edinburgh and a PhD in the breakdown of chemicals by bacteria from the University of Glasgow. He tweets as @mwarhurst.

CHAPTER 10

Oxfam's Humankind Index

Katherine Trebeck and Asha Abeyasekera

This chapter introduces Oxfam's Humankind Index – a tool developed to assess the collective prosperity of Scotland. It begins by outlining the political context that led to the conceptualization of the index, followed by an overview of the principles and values that underlined its development. The chapter describes the main ways in which the Humankind Index has been used in measuring Scotland's prosperity at both the national and community level, and discusses how it has been used as an advocacy tool with policy makers. It then reflects on the strengths and limitations of the Humankind Index and suggests ways in which it can potentially be adapted and used by other communities and groups beyond Scotland.

Keywords: wellbeing, collective prosperity, policy making, policy assessment, sustainable livelihoods

Introduction

Oxfam's Humankind Index for Scotland was devised to assess Scotland's prosperity through a holistic and more representative measure of progress than that provided by gross domestic product (GDP). The Humankind Index was specifically designed to move beyond the dominant economic model that relies on GDP as a determinant of a country's progress. It seeks to challenge this inadequate measure of economic growth, which allows little assessment of the quality and distribution of that growth. The Humankind Index focuses on measuring the real wealth of Scotland; in other words, by understanding what really matters to people, Oxfam's Humankind Index intends to uncover the conditions of wellbeing.

The Oxfam Humankind Index represents one of the first cases where a multidimensional measure of prosperity has been attempted for Scotland. It offers policy makers a new tool to measure Scotland's collective prosperity. Rather than being a top-down indicator like GDP, the Oxfam Humankind Index measures Scotland's overall prosperity based on the things that people said really mattered to them. Its development has already stimulated debate

http://dx.doi.org/10.3362/9781780448411.010

Box 10.1 Oxfam Scotland

Oxfam works to overcome poverty all over the world. Oxfam believes that poverty, social exclusion, and discrimination prevent people from exercising their full rights to, for example, housing, health care, education, and an adequate standard of living. Oxfam has been working in the UK since 1996: developing projects with people living in poverty to improve their lives and show how things can change; raising public awareness of poverty to create pressure for change; and working with policy makers to tackle the causes of poverty.

---

at various levels, from local community groups to policy makers, on how to foster and sustain a good life for all of the people of Scotland. Oxfam hopes that the Humankind Index will also enable more appropriate policy responses in the near future, as policies are taken to advance the priorities laid out in the Humankind Index.

Since 1996, Oxfam has worked with others to overcome poverty and suffering in Scotland. Through its work with communities, it became clear to Oxfam that the economic model that has dominated the UK for most of the last century has proved to be outdated, and that it has failed to sufficiently reduce poverty and address inequality. Despite decades of economic growth, regeneration, and antipoverty policies, many Scots continue to face a life characterized by high mortality, economic inactivity, mental and physical ill-health, poor educational attainment, and increasing exclusion from the dominant mode of economic development.[1] More than one in five children are in relative poverty (see the Humankind Index for 2012). Oxfam warns that in aiming for economic prosperity, the current economic model has largely ignored inequality in income and wealth, in life chances and lifestyles, and between individuals and communities.

Experiencing poverty in this rich country is also intensely stressful. Stigmatization through the media and political rhetoric adds to individuals' sense of anguish and isolation. People, not society, nor the economy, are blamed for their poverty. Meanwhile, pressures to consume abound in a culture that elevates status and image above relationships, community contribution, or care for the environment.

It has become clear that in pursuing economic growth without sufficient regard to its quality and distribution, we are chasing the wrong goal. Oxfam believes that to achieve sustainable livelihoods for all, we need to recognize the range of assets that are important to people. In order to take account of these assets, which together shape the prosperity of both individuals and communities, we need to better measure our country's progress both over time and within our communities.

To develop the Oxfam Humankind Index, Oxfam Scotland initiated a large-scale consultation process in 2011 working with a range of partners including the Craighead Institute, Northern Star, and the New Economics Foundation (NEF). This was a multi-stage process that engaged almost 3,000 people across Scotland. Oxfam made a particular effort to reach out to seldom-heard

---

Box 10.2 A pernicious paradox

Oxfam has found that in vulnerable communities the most important asset available to families and individuals is their family relationships and social networks. These social assets enable poor families and individuals to share resources, helping them to even out fluctuating fortunes and to cope in difficult circumstances.

Yet recent economic development in Scotland and the UK positions individuals as cheap, flexible labour – available when business needs them and expendable when it does not. This paradoxically relies on the crucial support systems in poor communities and, simultaneously, threatens to destroy them. For example, the ability to work long hours at short notice may only be possible because of good relations with neighbours who can help with childcare. Long hours and work patterns that are flexible for the employer, yet insecure for the employee, are ultimately likely to damage these vital support networks. Trust, relationships, and reciprocity are undermined by hyper-consumerism, status-driven consumption, and individual instant gratification through material acquisition, which are themselves driven by inequalities.

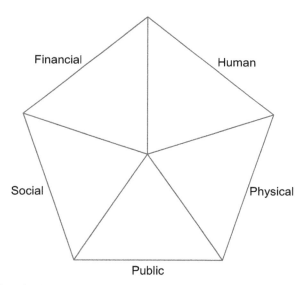

Figure 10.1 The livelihoods pentagon

communities, those groups whose interests are so often marginalized in the formal policy-making process and whose voices are absent from decisions that affect them. Mixed methods were deployed to engage with communities on their terms and in their spaces.

This participatory, deliberative, and inclusive consultation process was designed to arrive at a set of agreed priorities on what people need to live well in their communities. The discussion was framed using the **Sustainable Livelihoods Approach** (see Figure 10.1), which was augmented with other evidence regarding what is important to sustainability, prosperity, and wellbeing in Scotland.

Principles and values of the index

The underlying principle of the Oxfam Humankind Index is that *the economy should serve the people, not the other way around.* Its vision is to reposition the Scottish economy as the servant *of* the people and to pursue policies that deliver *for* the people. In doing so, it hopes to create a new prosperity with fewer extremes of money and wealth, esteem and status, and power and position. At the heart of this new prosperity would lie community-led economies that focus on the quality and distribution of growth – creating livelihoods for the many, not profits for the few. The assets of communities, and the value of individuals, would be utilized and enhanced to promote a sustainable and socially just future.

The primary objective of the consultative process was to construct, for the first time, an overall measure that adequately reflected the diverse priorities of the people living in Scotland. Because the Oxfam Humankind Index is about valuing the things that really matter to the people of Scotland, Oxfam asked the Scottish people about those aspects of life that make a real difference to them. The principles of **participation** and **inclusion** underlined the widespread public consultation. Oxfam made a particular effort to reach out to seldom-heard communities by deploying a range of consultative strategies, including focus groups, community workshops, street stalls, an online survey, and a representative poll.

These were skewed towards deprived communities and groups where people are disadvantaged by the formal, mainstream policy-making process. For example, many of the street stalls were held in areas of deprivation; focus groups were drawn from groups of disadvantage; and recruitment of participants for community meetings took place via organizations that worked with communities and groups whose voice Oxfam sought to elevate.

Oxfam also made an effort to reduce barriers to participation often faced by these communities – it provided childcare, reimbursed people for transport to and from meetings, and provided food and a gift certificate for those participants who were involved in events lasting over two hours.

Figure 10.2 The consultation process

Box 10.3 Asking the right questions

What do you need to live well in your community?
- What relationships are most important for a good life?
- What do you value about your community?
- What do you need for a good home life?
- What difference does education make to the chances of living a good life?
- What really matters when it comes to having money?
- What services do you think are most important for your community?
- What resources and assets are available to men and women in the community? What are the barriers?

An overview of the index

The range of views generated by the consultation were reviewed by the NEF, which constructed a weighted set of elements ('subdomains') that people reported as affecting their ability to live well in their communities. The final outcome of the consultation is shown in Figure 10.3.

The table defines a set of subdomains that outline the broad range of factors that people in Scotland believe are necessary to live well in their communities. Just as significantly, it also creates weightings for each of these that reflect their relative importance to Scottish people. This is one of the key results from the Oxfam Humankind Index project – it details a set of subdomains that those who took part in the consultation indicated as creating prosperity in their lives.

The composition of the Oxfam Humankind Index for Scotland is thus a reflection of the priorities of the people of Scotland. The table shows the relative importance of the various factors that people say are important to being able to live well in their communities. Some important findings are listed below:

- Housing and health are equally valued and both are valued more than other subdomains, such as having satisfying work or having the correct skills to live a good life.
- Living in a neighbourhood where you can enjoy going outside and having a clean and healthy environment is high on people's priorities, as are good relationships.
- Monetary factors are not people's top priority; sufficiency and security of income are more important than gross amounts. It further highlights that the quality of work (particularly work that is satisfying) is an important consideration.

Using the index to measure Scotland's prosperity

The subdomains defined by the people of Scotland as important factors in their prosperity were used in *four* main ways to measure Scotland's prosperity.

Oxfam Humankind Index

Order	Subdomain	Weighting
= 1	Affordable, decent and safe home	11
= 1	Physical and mental health	11
2	Living in a neighbourhood where you can enjoy going outside and having a clean and healthy environment	9
= 3	Having satisfying work to do (whether paid or unpaid)	7
= 3	Having good relationships with family and friends	7
= 4	Feeling that you and those you care about are safe	6
= 4	Access to green and wild spaces; community spaces and play areas	6
= 5	Secure work and suitable work	5
= 5	Having enough money to pay the bills and buy what you need	5
= 5	Having a secure source of money	5
= 5	Access to arts, hobbies and leisure activities	5
= 6	Having the facilities you need locally	4
= 6	Getting enough skills and education to live a good life	4
= 6	Being part of a community	4
= 6	Having good transport to get to where you need to go	4
7	Being able to access high-quality services	3
= 8	Human rights, freedom from discrimination, acceptance and respect	2
= 8	Feeling good	2

Figure 10.3 The Oxfam Humankind Index

1. Measuring collective prosperity

The primary objective was to construct the Oxfam Humankind Index itself, and to obtain for the first time an overall measure that adequately reflected the diverse priorities of people in Scotland. To do this, the subdomains were matched to existing Scottish data relating to the priorities identified. These were then used to calculate the overall Humankind Index for Scotland for a given time period.

The data sets describe whether people are satisfied with their position with respect to the relevant subdomain. For example, the Scottish Government's Scottish House Condition Survey was used in order to find out the percentage of people who reported that they were satisfied with their home and tallied with subdomain 1 – 'Affordable, decent and safe home'. For the subdomain 'Feeling that you and those you care about are safe', an approximation was derived from the Scottish Household Survey, which asks respondents whether they feel they live in a safe area, and the response for Scotland as a whole was entered into the main Humankind Index.

Where satisfaction measures were not available or appropriate, a relevant percentage was calculated. For example, the probability that an individual is in work was used to calculate a percentage for subdomain 8 – 'Secure work and suitable work' – but clearly this is far from a perfect proxy.

Finding data sets that perfectly represented the subdomains was one of the main challenges in constructing the Humankind Index. For example, subdomain 1 – 'Affordable, decent and safe home' – is intended to measure the satisfaction people obtain from the type of home they live in. The three attributes listed – affordability, standard, and security – presumably represent the most important qualities that people require from their home. There are difficulties in attempting to find one measure that satisfies all three of these requirements, and the data available was not sufficiently rich to provide an individual measure for each of these three key factors. Given this, an overall measure of people's satisfaction with their housing situation was used. This may not have strictly captured all three aspects of housing, but it does provide a sense of whether housing is satisfactory according to people's own priorities.

2. Measuring prosperity over time

A comparison of the index over time was also undertaken. Data limitations meant that consideration of only one time period was possible (between 2007–8 and 2009–10). Nonetheless, the difference in the index between these two years is of considerable interest because it appears to capture the influence of a deteriorating economy after 2008, yet it highlights that overall prosperity increased in 2009–10 despite lower economic activity in Scotland.

It is unfortunate that changes in data collection during the time period under review meant that the comparison could not track back further. However, a baseline has now been established that will allow measurement of the extent to which policy helps to meet people's priorities in the future.

3. Comparing prosperity in different communities

Given Oxfam's focus on tackling poverty in Scotland as a whole, comparing the index for deprived communities in Scotland against Scotland as a whole was crucial. The index clearly captured the substantial differences between deprived communities and all of Scotland, and also identified those areas where deprived communities suffer a deficit.

Overall, deprived communities score significantly below Scotland as a whole. Deprived areas had a measured prosperity (in terms of Humankind Index points) 10 per cent below the figure for Scotland as a whole. As mentioned before, the consultations revealed that a significant amount of the prosperity across all of Scotland relates to immediate local issues such as being able to enjoy going outside, living in a healthy environment, and the availability of green spaces and local amenities. Together, these contributed more than a third of the total weight of the index for all of Scotland.

It is therefore no great surprise that the main differences between deprived areas and the whole of Scotland occur with respect to neighbourhood subdomains. They accounted for just over 40 per cent of the difference between deprived communities and all of Scotland. People living in deprived communities are also less likely to feel they are part of a community, and overall the majority of the deficit thus arises from differences in the quality of life in the local area.

The index also picks up on differences in health, which account for 10 per cent of the difference in scores between deprived areas and the whole of Scotland. The other key difference is that deprived communities are more likely to struggle financially; this accounted for 16 per cent of the total gap compared with Scotland as a whole.

4. Considering prosperity in local authority areas

Oxfam also distilled the data in the Oxfam Humankind Index for all Scottish local authorities.[2] What is immediately obvious is the extent to which island and rural areas tend to have a higher score – of the 32 local authority areas in Scotland, the first three are island authorities, and the first seven are predominantly non-urban,[3] while the highest urban area is Edinburgh, which ranks eighth. This strongly suggests that a key reason why non-urban areas tend to perform so well is due to the quality of the local environment.

The major positive differences between the highest three areas (Shetland Islands, Eilean Siar, and Orkney) and the Scottish average for the relevant subdomains (as a percentage of all positive differences in all three areas) reveal three key trends:

- Environment does play an important role (see below), but the biggest difference is due to safety – all three of the highest-scoring areas show that people in these areas are considerably more likely to report that they live in a safe environment.[4]

HKI for Deprived Communities (2009–2010)

Variable	Weights	Measure	Score
Housing	11	50.2	537
Health	11	87.0	929
Neighbourhood/Environment	9	45.0	393
Work Satisfaction	7	70.8	496
Good Relationships	7	13.2	90
Safety	6	9.0	52
Green Spaces	6	32.5	189
Secure/Suitable Work	6	89.9	524
Having Enough Money	6	32.0	186
Financial Security	5	– 5.8	– 28
Culture/Hobbies	5	50.5	245
Local Facilities	4	41.0	159
Skills and Education	4	18.5	72
Community Spirit	4	58.0	225
Good Transport	4	80.4	312
Good Services	3	67.5	197
Tolerance	3	66.0	192
Feeling good	2	78.5	152

Total 4,923

Figure 10.4 The Humankind Index for deprived communities

- The visual appeal of these areas also appears to contribute to enhanced prosperity, given that the second major difference is the extent to which respondents reported feeling that they lived in a pleasant environment.
- Finally, all three areas report a higher incidence of community spirit. There also appears to be a positive, but smaller, influence from 'feeling good',

which may be related to the positive scores on the above subdomains. Greater satisfaction with housing also plays a role in two areas, although not in Shetland, where satisfaction with housing was below the Scottish average.[5]

Financial subdomains do not appear to make a very significant contribution to prosperity across local authorities. The three lowest-performing areas (North Lanarkshire, Glasgow, and East Ayrshire) all performed worse than Scotland on housing, health, neighbourhood/environment, safety, green spaces, having enough money, and community spirit. The key conclusion, as in our earlier discussion of deprivation, is that these areas perform poorly for a wide range of reasons and that there is no single reason, or set of reasons, why they do so badly. They are being dragged down by a range of factors.

Advocacy and coalition building

The Humankind Index has seen a growing body of third party support for the index itself as a way of assessing Scotland's 'real prosperity' and more broadly for the sort of questions it creates space to ask about Scotland's development model.

An informal coalition of supporters is growing among civil society organizations, and, to varying extents, they are undertaking their own advocacy for the Humankind Index. These organizations include several influential political commentators, such as WWF Scotland, the Scottish Trades Union Congress, the Scottish Council for Voluntary Organisations, Citizens Advice Scotland, the Scottish Environment Protection Agency, the Scottish Wildlife Trust, the Poverty Alliance, the Church of Scotland, Scottish Natural Heritage, Scotland's Futures Forum, and the Jimmy Reid Foundation.

The index has achieved significant media coverage at particular junctures, such as when it was launched, but also spontaneously as journalists make reference to the index in relation to other topics they are reporting. The Scottish Parliament Information Centre (SPICe) has twice referenced the Humankind Index in its briefings, including releasing a briefing on economic indicators (in which the Humankind Index was a 'guest indicator') to coincide with the launch of the Humankind Index. It has been frequently referenced in parliamentary debates, most recently by the then Scottish Labour Finance Minister to frame his contribution to a debate on under-employment.

As a result of agitation around the index by Oxfam and by policy makers in the Scottish Parliament, the Scottish Government has committed to seeking to improve Scotland's National Performance Framework, and Oxfam has been an invited guest at four roundtables on the National Performance Framework chaired by the Finance Minister.

The Scottish Labour Party has also shown significant interest in using the index to guide its policy development; the head of Oxfam Scotland was invited to talk about the index at the Labour Party conference. Several local authorities and public bodies have expressed interest in using the Humankind Index to shape policy and delivery.

A motion welcoming the Humankind Index received cross-party support from over a third of the members of the Scottish Parliament; this motion was then debated in the Scottish Parliament with all major parties contributing (to such an extent that extra time was required).

The then project lead has twice briefed the Scottish Economy, Energy and Tourism Committee, which then sought the views of Nobel-Prize-winning economist Professor Joseph Stiglitz on measures of progress (he described the Humankind Index as a job 'very well done' and commended Oxfam's efforts to create a civic conversation). Civil servants have sought Oxfam's input in policy development, where Oxfam was previously an outsider.

Oxfam Scotland has recently launched *Our Economy*. This report maps out Oxfam's perspective on the problems with the Scottish economy – in particular widening inequality – and proposes a range of potential solutions. The report received substantial coverage on its release and a member of the Scottish Parliament has already secured a parliamentary debate on the report in September 2014. The Humankind Index provides the basis (and credibility) through which Oxfam Scotland is able to call for a fairly radical restructuring of the Scottish economy.

Strengths and limitations

The major strengths of the Humankind Index are as follows:

- It was constructed by putting the voices of seldom-heard groups to the fore and consciously emphasizes the voices of people whose interests are marginalized in the formal policy-making process.
- It emphasizes collective prosperity, rather than individual wellbeing or happiness – it is not about creating a happiness or wellbeing index that simply aggregates each individual's assessment of their own satisfaction.
- It is participatory in its construction – people directly determined the composition of the index, as opposed to arbitrary weightings of components being nominated by think tanks or academics.
- It reveals the gap between deprived areas and the rest of the country, and identifies the nature and extent of that gap.
- It highlights measures that require improved data – those areas of life that Scottish people identify as being important to them, but that are currently insufficiently measured by government.

Limitations of the Humankind Index include the following:

- The consultation methods were constrained by a limited budget and time frame. To deliver the best results within these constraints, outreach was opportunistic, using Oxfam's existing networks rather than a large-scale comprehensive consultation.

- The collation of the results of the various survey events undertaken was iterative and involved some judgement, clustering, and translation of people's language and terminology. These are open to challenge.
- In seeking to highlight the voices of seldom-heard groups, there was a trade-off with the representativeness of the consultation results. Oxfam sought to mitigate this by commissioning a representative poll of a representative sample of over 1,000 Scottish people, which, according to the index's methods advisers and steering group, showed that the consultation 'adequately reflected' the views of the Scottish people.
- By emphasizing the participatory construction of the Humankind Index, the scope to compare the results with other countries is reduced. A similar consultation in another context might yield very different domains, and so the cross-country comparability would be undermined. This was acknowledged by Oxfam from the start – the decision was taken that participation was more important than competition and comparison between countries. It was also felt that trends over time could be compared if deemed necessary.
- In bringing together the data in a single number – comprising the weighted domains – Oxfam made a strategic choice that this would aid publicity, particularly garnering media attention. There are valid criticisms of such a composite index; however, in also providing a set of domains (a 'dashboard' that critics of a single number often call for) and in weighting them according to people's preferences, Oxfam's approach offers several products that can be used for different purposes and modes of analysis.

As Oxfam makes clear, there are problems with the data available for collation of the index – the data needed to be able to be broken down by year, local authority, gender, and area of deprivation. This restricted the available sources, and some rather problematic proxies were used. It is hoped that the knowledge base will improve over time and that the Humankind Index will similarly be able to be improved as better data becomes available.

Using the Oxfam Humankind Index beyond Scotland

The purpose of this section is to provide an overview of how Oxfam's Humankind Index can be potentially adapted to different contexts and replicated with other communities. While we acknowledge that the Oxfam Humankind Index reflects the specific needs and priorities of the Scottish people, and was specifically designed to assess prosperity in Scotland, we believe that the index and tools developed can be used by policy makers and non-governmental organizations outside Scotland for understanding and assessing wellbeing in other policy contexts and local settings.

How and to what extent the Oxfam Humankind Index and its related tools are replicated and used by institutions and organizations will depend on two main factors, namely their needs and priorities, as well as on the resources available for assessment. We anticipate engagement at three different levels.

1. 'A light touch': the online tool for assessing policy

The Humankind Index policy assessment tool operationalizes the Humankind Index by examining the impact of policies on the 18 elements of the index. It is an online tool that asks whether certain courses of action will contribute positively or negatively to the various priorities. It prompts users to consider the impact of a policy on various groups that can sometimes be overlooked in decision making. In doing so, it aims to ensure that a much broader range of factors are given proper consideration during policy design and development. It also expands thinking about the range of impacts a policy may have on people's ability to live well in their communities. The tool is available at <http://policytool.humankindindex.org/>.

2. Medium engagement: using the existing index created in Scotland for an audience outside Scotland

Instead of starting an open-ended discussion about what factors contribute to wellbeing, this would basically mean using the existing 18 subdomains derived from the consultation process to initiate a discussion. People can rank the subdomains according to their needs and priorities. While coming up with weights and measures requires the involvement of experts, a simple ranking exercise would still provide an overview of what people think is important to their wellbeing.

3. Deeper engagement: replicating the process to derive locally specific factors of prosperity

In India, for example, Oxfam is drawing on the methodology developed in Scotland to engage with disadvantaged communities about what sort of development they want to see. Plans are being made to use the results of these participatory conversations to create a tool to assess policies and to develop a vision for India's future development. Furthermore, discussions are under way with partners and funders to develop a Humankind Index for the United Kingdom.

Endnotes

1. See the Oxfam discussion paper *Whose Economy?* (January 2011) at <http://policy-practice.oxfam.org.uk/publications/whose-economy-winners-and-losers-in-the-new-scottish-economy-118965> [accessed 24 June 2014].
2. The Humankind Index is available at <http://policy-practice.oxfam.org.uk/blog/2012/05/~/media/25D330EF80F343B8977A00FECDF98FEF.ashx> [accessed 24 June 2014].
3. The recently declared city of Perth is obviously included in Perth and Kinross.

4. This is the area response reported in Table 4.3 of the Scottish household survey, 'Aspects of neighbourhood particularly liked'. In Shetland, 68 per cent of respondents reported that they lived in a safe environment.
5. However, the actual difference here is relatively minor – 54 per cent of people in Scotland were satisfied with the quality of housing compared with 51.6 per cent in Shetland.

Katherine Trebeck is the Research and Policy Adviser on Oxfam GB's Research Team, where she is exploring an economy that delivers social justice, good lives, and vibrant communities, and which protects the planet. She has been at Oxfam since 2005 working as Policy and Advocacy Manager for Oxfam's UK programme, and prior to this she was Research and Policy Adviser for Oxfam's Scotland work. Here she developed Oxfam's Humankind Index and managed Oxfam's Whose Economy? project, which asked why, despite decades of economic growth, Scotland's poverty has not been addressed and inequalities have deepened. She has a PhD in political science from the Australian National University.

Asha Abeyasekera is a lecturer at the Faculty of Graduate Studies, University of Colombo, Sri Lanka. She has worked for more than 10 years as a practitioner and researcher in the development sector, focusing mainly on gender-related issues and psychosocial work. She was one of the lead researchers and Programme Manager of the Psychosocial Assessment of Development and Humanitarian Interventions (PADHI) project (2006–9). She received her PhD from the University of Bath.

CHAPTER 11

Wellbeing Wales: the Sustainable Wellbeing Framework

Dafydd Thomas

This chapter introduces the Sustainable Wellbeing Framework which was developed for the Welsh Government in discussion with members of the Wellbeing Wales Network, and describes the political impetus for its development. After introducing the principal components of the framework, the chapter explains how the framework, as well as the Exploring Sustainable Wellbeing Toolkit, can be used to develop and evaluate public policies and programmes. Two case studies are then presented to illustrate how the information generated from the toolkit was helpful in evaluating the wider impact of existing public policy programmes in Wales, and also some of the challenges of incorporating the findings into practice.

Keywords: sustainable wellbeing, policy impact assessment, monitoring and evaluation, policy development

Introduction

Lles Cymru Wellbeing Wales, previously known as the Wellbeing Wales Network, was established in 2004 by a number of voluntary organizations in response to an emergent strategic context where wellbeing was increasingly referred to in Welsh policy development and discourse. In simple terms, a number of individuals and groups could see wellbeing rising up the policy ladder, but they were unsure about what they could do about it.

The Welsh Government's wellbeing approach was articulated in the consultation paper *Better Health Better Wales* (Welsh Office, 1998), which stated that the government wanted to 'improve the health and wellbeing of the people of Wales'. With strategies such as *A Winning Wales* (Welsh Assembly Government, 2001), the Welsh Government was laying the groundwork to support a wider approach to promoting wellbeing. This noted that 'increasing GDP does not automatically lead to better quality of life for our people. The way we develop is important too.' In 2002, another consultation document – *Wellbeing in Wales* (Welsh Assembly Government, 2002) – saw wellbeing as a

http://dx.doi.org/10.3362/9781780448411.011

'core aim around which a concerted effort [could] be developed across policy areas'. Despite the favourable policy environment, practical suggestions on how to increase wellbeing were not being clearly articulated from within the Welsh Government. What also was not clear was how these different discussions on wellbeing could be linked in a way that would influence overall thinking within the Welsh public service sector.

Opportunities were presenting themselves at the local level too. A unique Welsh policy process was being rolled out, stipulating that local authorities and their partners should co-operatively develop 'local health, social care, and wellbeing strategies'. According to the Welsh Assembly Government's *Health, Social Care and Well-being Strategies: Policy Guidance*, 'Well-being provides a strong test of the extent to which policies are coming together to reduce inequalities and to promote sustainable development. A high-level of well-being is a feature of strong and vibrant communities' (Welsh Assembly Government, 2003).

In 2004, the then Wellbeing Wales Network aimed to join up these different ad-hoc wellbeing activities and policy across Wales. It sought to help make the concept of wellbeing something quite practical that organizations could plan for, deliver, and eventually measure. The key to making these changes was the Sustainable Wellbeing Framework. The framework was developed by the New Economics Foundation in discussion with the Welsh Government and members of the Wellbeing Wales Network.

The Sustainable Wellbeing Framework

The Sustainable Wellbeing model is based on four components:

- physical and psychological wellbeing;
- economic and material wellbeing;
- community and society wellbeing;
- environmental wellbeing.

These four components provide an 'entry point' into discussions about sustainable wellbeing, so that participants develop an understanding of wellbeing in their own terms.

Using the model can help people make the links between different attributes of the policy or project under consideration. The basic principle is that a focus on one priority does not happen in isolation. For example, teaching someone to cycle not only means that they have learned a new skill and are able to celebrate that fact. It also means that they have a means of independent travel. Furthermore, they may meet other cyclists and benefit from that social interaction. They may also exercise more on a regular basis, shed excess weight, and improve their health. The list goes on. As illustrated in this example, the initial project aim to teach someone to cycle can have many and varied consequences, which can also have a wider wellbeing impact.

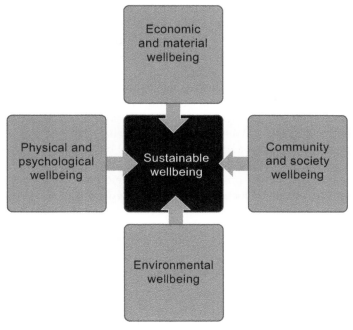

Figure 11.1 The Sustainable Wellbeing model used by the Wellbeing Wales Network

The framework also places a strong emphasis on how society's environmental impact is a fundamental factor in sustainable wellbeing. This resonated deeply with members of the Wellbeing Wales Network, many of whom were from environmental organizations, and it had obvious links with the Welsh Government's statutory duty to promote sustainable development.[1]

Using the Sustainable Wellbeing Framework to develop and evaluate policy

In 2008–9, the Wellbeing Wales Network co-ordinator wanted to engage the target audience in a wider discussion about what wellbeing meant to different people, without using an explicit definition. The Sustainable Wellbeing Framework promoted such a discussion. It was a deliberate tactic to help generate as much interest as possible around the topic of wellbeing by being as inclusive as possible – although it could have been somewhat problematic for pragmatic organizations more comfortable with specific definitions and targets.

The Sustainable Wellbeing Framework encourages its user to see how various issues connect with one another. To use the same example of cycling, the aim of a particular project could be to increase the numbers cycling in a particular community. In terms of measures of success, funders and also local and national governments might use more traditional targets, like the number of people taking part on a course or the overall distance cycled. The Sustainable Wellbeing Framework helps an organization understand all the layers of issues around a proposed outcome. In encouraging people to ride a bike, a project can potentially help individuals combat isolation, boost low participant confidence, and improve poor physical health, as well as helping those taking part learn a new skill. The Sustainable Wellbeing Framework challenges policy makers and project managers to adopt a different perspective: by looking at clients from a different point of view, they would, ideally, work differently with them as well.

Client participation in project or policy development is something that most members of the Wellbeing Wales Network encourage, and participation is a unifying theme in all their work. As a consequence, looking at outcomes through the lens of sustainable wellbeing encourages new discussions about how a project or policy might impact on clients or partners in a way that would not have happened before.

The Sustainable Wellbeing Framework has been used:

- to stimulate discussion about wellbeing using the first module of the Exploring Sustainable Wellbeing Toolkit;
- as the basis for the development of guidance on how to operationalize wellbeing;[2]
- as the basis for developing an assessment process for policy, strategy, and consultation documents;
- as the basis for a summative assessment of participant or user inner wellbeing;
- to identify different ways of measuring a project's success or impact.

In summary, the Sustainable Wellbeing Framework promotes a richer understanding of a project or policy's impact. This understanding can then be used to measure success and inform the policy or project's further development. This is demonstrated in the example below.

When Wellbeing Wales carried out a wellbeing assessment of a large corporation's staff health and welfare policies, it became apparent that the policy of the organization towards staff wellbeing was comprehensive and very commendable. Unfortunately, these ambitious policies were not being communicated effectively to the staff, nor were they being properly translated into positive action. Using the Sustainable Wellbeing Framework, Wellbeing Wales was able to generate a productive discussion. Talking with staff members about their wellbeing really encouraged the participants to open up, and the framework enabled them to make the links between the different issues that were affecting their wellbeing in the workplace. Ironically, the organization's leadership did not know how to respond to the integrated feedback that the wellbeing assessment generated. Even though they had commissioned this piece of work to understand how things fitted together in terms of wellbeing, they eventually resorted to a single-issue approach when it came to addressing the problems, such as health checks to tackle high blood pressure in the workplace.

The Exploring Sustainable Wellbeing Toolkit

The Exploring Sustainable Wellbeing Toolkit was developed to help individuals and organizations operationalize the Sustainable Wellbeing Framework during the planning phase of a project – when an organization is working out what it wants to do and with whom. The toolkit can also benefit organizations when the project is well into its delivery stage as a review of progress.

For the Exploring Sustainable Wellbeing Toolkit to be effective, between 4 and 10 participants are needed. These participants should reflect as wide a range of project stakeholders as possible. This group should include people who you think have an interest in the project. You could prioritize who to invite by thinking of the people who *must* be there, the people who *should* be involved, and finally the people who *could* be invited.

The toolkit lets users ask their own questions about what they are learning about wellbeing and how to apply it to their work. The toolkit is a modular process and is broken down into the following sections:

- **Understanding sustainable wellbeing:** In this stage the aim is to get the toolkit users to discuss the four elements of wellbeing. What do these ideas really mean to them? The sort of questions asked could include: What does the jargon really mean to them? How do these different issues join up? What are the priorities? What parts of their work do they feel comfortable with? What parts of their work are more challenging? Why is that? How do things link up?

  By the end of this stage, the participants will have a series of words they have come up with to describe their project in terms of sustainable wellbeing.
- **Where are we now?** Having discussed what the four elements of sustainable wellbeing mean for the project under discussion, the group of users now needs to assess the impact the project is likely to have on the four elements highlighted in the framework. Alternatively, during a project review, this stage could be used to understand the impact the project has had so far.

  The sort of questions asked at this stage could include: What needs to change? What is going well? What isn't doing quite so well? Why isn't it? What is the evidence for that? What do our users think? Where would they like to see change?
- **What could we do better?** The objective of this stage is to get participants to brainstorm ideas that might improve the project's impact on sustainable wellbeing. The previous section focuses on generating an honest appraisal of what is being considered. There are no questions at

this stage, and therefore there are no wrong answers, only suggestions from the toolkit users as to what could be done to improve their project or plan – a bit of 'blue sky' thinking.

- **Where do we want to be?** The group's ideas on what needs to happen to change the project so that it can have the greatest positive impact on community or individual wellbeing should be deliberated at this stage. The long list of ideas generated in the previous section should be organized depending on their impact. Those with the least wellbeing impact, as decided by the participants in the process, should be discarded. The long list of ideas can then be converted to a more manageable shortlist of actions the group can take forward with its project.

  More questions are asked again at this stage, and the viability and impact of the suggested changes to the project should be discussed with the objective of doing a few things well after a process of prioritization. This stage also helps participants make choices about what is desirable and, at the same time, viable and practical.

- **Evaluation and interpretation:** This final stage has two objectives. Firstly, as this is a participative process, it is important to capture immediate feedback on what the toolkit's users think of the process. Secondly, in refining the project using the toolkit, it is important to identify what kind of quantitative data or user testimony could be used to measure the impact of the proposed changes to the project in the long term.

Case studies: sustainable wellbeing model as the basis of a wellbeing assessment

The Garw Valley Weight Management Programme

The Garw Valley Weight Management Programme was developed to manage and support obese patients currently registered with a local doctors' practice by providing them with an easily accessible, community-based weight management programme. The programme links up activities, groups, and initiatives that already exist within the community as a means to help the participants manage their own weight.

Those who attended the Weight Management Programme were encouraged to attend a series of focus groups to share their experiences of taking part in the scheme. This included talking about what had worked well from their perspective as participants within the programme, and also about the things that did not work quite so well. The Sustainable Wellbeing Framework was used to make sense of these group discussions. After the main issues were identified, a questionnaire was developed. This was circulated to those who had been and were currently participants on the programme. Nearly 300 responses were then analysed as part of the assessment.

The programme's designers wanted to encourage the participants to walk or cycle more when travelling locally as a way of controlling their weight. By using the framework to make sense of the participants' experiences, it became clear that the commissioners of the Weight Management Programme had not considered the impact that poverty was having on people's food choices. It was also found that worrying about money was having a big impact on a person's ability to manage their weight. In such a context, going for local walks to keep one's weight off was not something that many of the participants had really thought about or were even interested in.

However, while the assessment identified that the economic and material wellbeing of the participants was having the biggest impact, it could not differentiate between the different aspects within these areas. Were the limitations of the household budget undermining participant wellbeing? Or was it the lack of access to different food choices?

The information generated from the wellbeing assessment was fed back to the commissioning team. Upon reflection, it seemed obvious that in a deprived community some consideration should have been given to the impact that limited financial resources had on participants' lifestyle choices. This highlights how the Sustainable Wellbeing Framework can help the commissioners of services or the designers of policy take a step back and have a more integrated view of issues that confront them.

National Federation of Women's Institutes' 'Get Cooking' project

The Women's Institute (WI) has been running the 'Get Cooking' programme in Wales since 1992. The programme aims to help women with young families cook nutritious and appetizing meals while still living within the confines of a tight household budget. As part of the programme, the Institute's volunteers run a six-week cooking course for parents from a particular school. The course itself is run within local community venues in order to make it easy for people to attend and also to foster a sense of belonging to a 'community' among the participants. While learning how to cook nutritious meals, participants on the 'Get Cooking' programme get to spend time with each other and make new friends during the course. According to Lisa Howells, the programme co-ordinator, the programme teaches participants 'how to cook on a low budget, and how to get the best out of their cooking, to make cooking fun, and to involve the whole family in cooking'.

Organizers of the programme have known for some time that there was more to this project than cooking. As the head of the National Federation of Women's Institutes in Wales, Rhian Connick, observed: 'The WI has a fine history of providing local responses to national concerns, such as obesity and climate change, so we wanted to see if we could include that in the evolution of the project.' The Exploring Sustainable Wellbeing Toolkit was, therefore, used to analyse the wider impacts of the programme. This brought attention to environmental issues which had not been considered before. The organizers responded by deciding to incorporate environmental messages in the programme. As a result, the WI now includes fact sheets on seasonal foods, food miles, recycling, and energy saving with the programme.

Lessons learned

On reflection, the value of the Sustainable Wellbeing Framework is that it provides an entry point and a relatively simple way to think about wellbeing in a specific context or with a particular group of people. The first stage of the Exploring Sustainable Wellbeing Toolkit – understanding wellbeing – can be used, for example, as a stand-alone process to help its users get a better appreciation of wellbeing.

The framework, particularly when used with the Exploring Sustainable Wellbeing Toolkit, gives participants a chance to step back, think about their work, and look at increasing their wellbeing impact. It helps people see the connections between various issues and concerns. It can help identify benchmarks for progress, common ground with other initiatives, and potential new partners.

Many of the organizations who have used the toolkit have found its flexibility very useful, and have been able to adapt it for their specific needs. For example, the See Change project run by Interlink in Rhondda Cynon Taff has used the Sustainable Wellbeing model as a way to discuss social enterprises in the county. The Environment Agency Wales used the cards from the toolkit to start discussions with external partners about their work.

The Sustainable Wellbeing Framework and the toolkit have fulfilled their strategic role of raising awareness about wellbeing at the policy and practical level. And they will continue to increase the contribution of their users to improving wellbeing, wherever that may be.

Endnotes

1. This is covered by the Government of Wales Act 2006, Section 79.
2. The Sustainable Wellbeing Framework has been used to inform the following publications: *How to Promote Wellbeing in Communities*; *How to Promote Wellbeing in Policy*; *Exploring Sustainable Wellbeing Toolkit*; *The First Incomplete Guide to Wellbeing in Wales*; 12 responses to Welsh Government consultations on national and local policies and strategies; and evaluations of two rounds of 22 Welsh local authority health, social care, and wellbeing strategies in both 2009 and 2012. This information was then used to inform the Welsh Government's guidance to local authorities on how to compile their own health, social care, and wellbeing strategies.

References

Welsh Assembly Government (2001) *A Winning Wales: The National Economic Development Strategy of the Welsh Assembly Government*, Cardiff: National Assembly for Wales. <www.rctcbc.gov.uk/en/relateddocuments/publications/developmentplanning/examination/examinationlibrary/walesdocuments/

w3-awinningwalesthenationaleconomicdevelopmentstrategyofthewag.pdf> [accessed 24 June 2014].

Welsh Assembly Government (2002) *Wellbeing in Wales: Consultation Document*, Cardiff: Welsh Assembly Government. <www.wales.nhs.uk/ documents/file1-full-doc-e.pdf> [accessed 24 June 2014].

Welsh Assembly Government (2003) *Health, Social Care and Well-being Strategies: Policy Guidance*, Cardiff: Welsh Assembly Government. <http://wales.gov.uk/topics/health/publications/health/strategies/ strategies/?lang=en> [accessed 24 June 2014].

Welsh Office (1998) *Better Health Better Wales*, Cardiff: Welsh Office. <www. wales.nhs.uk/publications/greenpaper98_e.pdf> [accessed 24 June 2014].

Dafydd Thomas is the co-founder of Lles Cymru Wellbeing Wales – a charity aimed at integrating wellbeing outcomes into Welsh Government policies and projects. He started his career as a campaign volunteer with Friends of the Earth and later worked closely with community groups in Wales on local and global environmental issues. Subsequently, he has managed a number of programmes that put policy aspiration into practice, including helping individuals to make healthier choices, supporting community groups as they engage in democratic processes, and challenging organizations to become more environmentally aware. He has a BSc in marine biology and an MSc in applied oceanography from the University of Wales. <uk.linkedin.com/in/ dafyddthomas1>

PART FOUR

Going forward

CHAPTER 12

Conclusion: the politics of working on wellbeing

Sarah C. White

This chapter considers the politics of working on wellbeing, happiness, and quality of life at a national and international level. It considers the use of national and international wellbeing indices and the scope of happiness and wellbeing to provide alternative models of development. It then considers some of the main critiques, which are used to argue against focusing on wellbeing in policy contexts. It closes by setting out some key principles to guide the use of wellbeing assessment in policy and practice.

Keywords: politics of wellbeing, wellbeing indices, development ethics

Introduction

This book has focused on the practicalities of working on wellbeing or quality of life at the project or programme level and the use of wellbeing in advocating for policy change. In this concluding chapter we locate this in the broader context: What are the politics of working on wellbeing? And what transformative potential does it have at the national and international level?

Wellbeing in national and international indices

As mentioned in Chapter 1, there is widespread interest in measuring wellbeing at national and international level. An increasing number of national governments are adopting some measures of subjective wellbeing in official surveys. Canada, Australia, and New Zealand were forerunners in this, joined in 2011 by the UK Office for National Statistics' adoption of four subjective wellbeing questions as part of its regular Integrated Household Survey.[1] The Organisation for Economic Co-operation and Development (OECD, 2013) reports France, Italy, the United States, the Netherlands, Japan, and South Korea as also either measuring or planning to measure wellbeing at a national level.

http://dx.doi.org/10.3362/9781780448411.012

In addition, a growing number of academic and commercial enterprises gather data on subjective wellbeing internationally. These build on smaller-scale academic studies dating back to the 1960s. The World Values Survey led the way in 1981; the European Social Survey has asked about life satisfaction since 2004; and the Gallup World Poll was launched in 2005. The consistent methodology and volume of people covered by the World Poll mean that the Gallup life satisfaction measure is now by far the most influential source of data on subjective wellbeing globally. Gallup is also a strong actor in the field, advocating life satisfaction (expressed in terms of 'thriving') along with the percentage of the population in formal employment as the 'two metrics ... most valuable for world leaders to track and target' (Krogmeier et al., 2012).

The primary purpose of national statistics is to inform the government – and perhaps the people – of how a country is doing overall, and how different regions or sectors of the population are faring within this. Beyond this, however, a major use of this data is to form indices that rank countries against one another. These join established measures that are published annually, such as the World Bank's World Development Indicators and the United Nations Development Programme's (UNDP's) Human Development Index. They share dissatisfaction with gross domestic product (GDP) as an overall measure of national progress and the conviction that other dimensions need to be taken into account. They differ from previous indices in including both subjective and objective variables.

The New Economic Foundation's Happy Planet Index (2006 onwards) provides the most straightforward measure. Placing the major emphasis on environmental sustainability, it ranks countries by a simple formula:[2]

$$\text{Happy Planet Index} \quad = \quad \frac{\text{life satisfaction} \ \times \ \text{life expectancy}}{\text{ecological footprint}}$$

Alternative measures take a multi-domain approach. The OECD's Better Life Index (2011 onwards) identifies 11 domains of wellbeing, which together reflect 'material living conditions' and 'quality of life'.[3] The website stresses that it does not provide a ranking, but offers an interactive web tool that allows users to assign their own weights to domains, and so see how countries rank against one another according to which domain is viewed as being more or less important. The Legatum Institute's Prosperity Index (2010 onwards) ranks countries according to eight sub-indices, again intended to reflect two key dimensions: wealth and wellbeing.[4] The Social Progress Index was launched in 2013, combining 52 indicators of three dimensions: 'basic human needs', 'foundations of wellbeing', and 'opportunity'.[5]

While they appear to be offering data in an open-handed way,[6] the purpose of these indices is political: the incentive of moving up the ranking is intended to shift policy in a particular direction. In some cases this is quite explicit. nef, for example, states:

The HPI [Happy Planet Index] demonstrates that the dominant Western model of development is not sustainable and we need to find other development paths towards sustainable well-being. (nef, 2014)

Similarly, the Global Agewatch Index of Help Age International is openly designed to advance advocacy of the needs and rights of older people. The Social Progress Index 'hopes to put social and environmental considerations at the top of the policy and corporate agenda' (Confino, 2013).

The advocacy agendas of other indices may be less explicit, but nonetheless exist. The Legatum Institute and Gallup organization, for example, may be formally non-aligned, but they share a strong commitment to individual liberty, prosperity, and entrepreneurialism as the engine of growth.

While the various indices have different purposes and orientations, they also share some points in common. All of the indices discussed in this section are expert-led and are based in – and draw on scholarship from – wealthy countries, especially the USA and northern Europe. They all identify wellbeing and happiness in individualistic terms. Despite the democratic appeal of interactive websites that provide free information in a user-friendly form, they all rely on the advanced manipulation of statistics, which makes it hard for ordinary people to evaluate the conclusions they draw.

Happiness, living well, and development alternatives

Ideas of wellbeing are also used to argue for a different philosophy of development. The idea of 'gross national happiness' as a culturally grounded alternative to GDP originated with the King of Bhutan in the 1970s. In 2011, in response to a resolution from Bhutan, the United Nations recognized the 'pursuit of happiness' as a fundamental human goal and invited member states to develop happiness and human wellbeing measures that can be used to guide public policy.[7] Although the links with Bhutan have been important in symbolic terms, bringing associations of Eastern spiritual authenticity and more collectivist values, the advancement of happiness as a world agenda has been very much a collaborative effort. The first 'World Happiness Report' (Helliwell et al., 2012) was edited by three economics professors from North America and the UK: John Helliwell, Richard Layard, and Jeffrey Sachs. With a view to influencing the debates about what should follow the Millenium Development Goals, an international team of global 'experts' subsequently produced a 'new development paradigm' published by the Government of Bhutan in December 2013 (NDP Steering Committee and Secretariat, 2013). This seeks to draw on some elements that are held to reflect a distinctive Bhutanese worldview, emphasizing living in joy and harmony with the natural world, preserving cultural heritage and values, and an orientation towards service rather than personal gain. The report's core orientation, however, is definitely global rather than local. It contains much that is familiar from the section above, drawing heavily on happiness economics, positive psychology, and subjective wellbeing approaches. This includes a quite individualistic understanding of happiness, which needs to be fostered through 'happiness skills', and a strong emphasis on measurement and indicators.

The philosophy of *buen vivir* or *vida plena* ('living well' or 'fulfilled life') in Latin America represents a more profoundly alternative approach. Unlike all the other approaches discussed in this book, it has arisen through a bottom-up process of political mobilization, a rights-based struggle of disenfranchised people that combines leftist politics with indigenous worldviews. These emphasize the claims of the natural world and environmental sustainability, the need for redistribution and expanded state welfare provision, and the collective rights of marginalized peoples to inclusion within a state that recognizes within it the equal rights of a plurality of cultures and nations. A frontal assault on neoliberal policies and values, *buen vivir* has been enshrined within the constitutions of Ecuador and Bolivia. Paradoxically, this coexists with heavy dependence on mining and oil extraction with high environmental costs. The extent to which it can result in genuinely different policies and practice depends on the daily politics of reforming state structures, and the extent to which space can be made within international relations for a radically distinctive economic model.[8]

Reading global indices

How, then, should we approach the global indices on wellbeing? The answer is: with caution. What is most important is to look behind the labels, to read beyond the headlines, so that you can sift out the data from its packaging into particular claims. The following are some points that may help guide you in this process.

- Global indices all share an important limitation: they can work only with statistics that are available. The indices are not generating new measures, but simply collating data that already exists. This can result in slippage between the concept and the indicator that is said to measure it. For example, if many transactions take place 'off the books' in the informal economy, official measures will underestimate the amount of economic activity actually taking place. The further you go from 'traditional' statistical indicators, the less likely you are to find a regularly and reliably gathered set of figures common to a large number of countries. This can lead to relying on proxies, leaving room for debate as to whether the data sources are valid indicators for what they are claiming to show.
- To make a big statement you have to simplify. There is often room to question the way in which items are grouped together to make up a domain, for example. How good is the fit? What is the logic behind it? However much the data is presented as 'speaking for itself', in fact it always comes in a form that is pre-digested and shaped in ways that tell a particular story.
- Just as the indices are all selling some kind of narrative about how the world is and should be, they are also, of course, selling themselves.

Some of the claims that are made can therefore simply be discounted as marketing speak. That there are now so many competing indices may be seen as a good thing – it shows that there are alternatives and makes it hard for any to have the last word.

- Nevertheless, some of the statements are distinctly 'Big Brotherish', if also far-fetched. Gallup's claims that it 'gives leaders a scientific window into the thoughts and behaviours of 98% of the world's adult population', and that this can let the leaders know 'if their governments are at risk of being toppled by a revolution', would seem to fit in this category (Robison, 2012). In one way, of course, this is nothing new. CIA factsheets and Economist Intelligence Unit country reports provide well-established brief résumés of country profiles according to global templates. Where the data presented is becoming increasingly personal and intimate, however, it seems particularly important to pay attention to the politics of its generation and use.

Critiques of wellbeing

As emphasized in the opening chapters, it is important to pay attention to the politics of how wellbeing and quality of life are being used. Critics – like the advocates – represent both the right and left of the political spectrum. In this section we consider some of the main points that are raised *against* focusing on wellbeing or quality of life in policy contexts.

- *Too intrusive*. The concern that the more expansive approach of wellbeing can be personally intrusive is raised in the introductory chapters. It can also be seen more politically: to what extent should people's personal lives be subject to the surveillance or intervention of the state?
- *Too personal*. The objection that the personal focus of wellbeing makes it inappropriate as a policy target takes a number of different forms. How far is it the government's business to make people happy? To what extent is the sense of wellbeing affected by social policy in any case, since it depends so heavily on very local, personal factors? Or again, is wellbeing or quality of life an appropriate focus only at the level of an individual or small community – can subjective data meaningfully be 'scaled up'.
- *De-politicizing*. Some warn that the focus on individual experience can divert attention from tangible needs and rights. Others are concerned about the emphasis on individual responsibility. On the one hand, this can suggest that you are responsible for your own happiness, and so justify the withdrawal of state support. On the other hand, it can discourage political action – happiness lies not in changing the world but in how you feel about the world (or even in how you feel about yourself!).
- *Interpreting results*. Subjective wellbeing indicators in particular are criticized as being transient, shallow, and easily manipulated. Since some cultures encourage self-promotion while others value modesty, average

scores cannot simply be compared between countries and assumed to reflect real differences in quality of life. Also, while there is a growth in panel data that tracks the same individuals over time, there is still widespread dependence on reading causal connections into correlations. This leaves space for politically very different diagnoses, and policies that result from them. For example, there is widely found to be a correlation between low subjective wellbeing and unemployment. But are people unhappy because they are unemployed, or unemployed because they are unhappy? The numbers alone cannot answer this – it calls for more detailed, qualitative data on the processes involved.

- *Substance.* This criticism is directed particularly at the emphasis on 'happiness'. As already discussed, many maintain that subjective wellbeing constitutes a very limited way to evaluate human wellbeing. Some argue that people's values and choices are better expressed by what they do than by what they say (what economists call 'revealed preferences'). Philosophers also have criticized the 'tyranny of the positive attitude' (Held, 2002), arguing that pressure constantly to emphasize the sunny side can be highly ideological, and sadness can be important for mental health.
- *Composite indicators.* Some also argue against multidimensional approaches that combine different items within a single measure. They maintain that composite measures provide poor diagnostics from which to direct action – you do not know which component is actually making the difference.
- *Cross-cutting issues.* The breadth of wellbeing also brings a critical political dilemma: while it is everybody's business, by the same token it is nobody's responsibility. In the practical politics of government, finance tends to be allocated by sector or by specific ministries, leaving overarching issues (such as gender or wellbeing) chronically short of implementation power.

Working to *promote* wellbeing: Appadurai's 'capacity to aspire'

The anthropologist Arjun Appadurai's (2004) study of the 'capacity to aspire' brings out a very different possibility for working with wellbeing in projects, programmes, and social movements. Focusing on people's aspirations – their hopes and desires for a better life – can become a way of *promoting* wellbeing, not just assessing it: enabling people to move closer to where they would like to be, rather than simply evaluating where they are. This turns on its head the observation made in Chapter 2, that it is difficult to monitor wellbeing over time because people tend to change the standards by which they judge how they are doing ('moving goalposts'). Appadurai's argument is that the goalposts should be the target, and that a key aim of projects and social movements should be to expand people's horizons and to enhance their capacities to achieve the better life that they desire.

Appadurai begins by stressing the role of culture and social interaction in keeping poor people poor, as habits of thought, speech, and behaviour confirm and reproduce existing patterns of advantage and disadvantage. He gives the example of 'untouchable' castes in India, whose degraded social status is reinforced through every exchange with so-called 'higher' castes. Like Paulo Freire (1972) before him, Appadurai thus identifies cultural action as a potential space of resistance and empowerment.

Next, he argues that 'the capacity to aspire' is a cultural capacity, shared within social groups. He describes it further as a 'navigational capacity', meaning that what matters is not only knowing what you want, but also knowing how to get there. Then, he argues that the capacity to aspire is less developed in less advantaged people than in more advantaged individuals. This does not mean that poorer people do not hope for a better life or have ideas about how they want to advance, but that the 'map' of alternatives they can envisage and their understanding of how to reach them will be less varied, less detailed, and less reliable than those of richer people, who have a wealth of connections with knowledge of a greater range of options and experience of achieving them. For example, a child from a poor family and a child from a rich family may both dream of being a doctor one day. But the child from the rich family is much more likely to have the resources at home to allow her to stay at school; have family or friends who are doctors whom she can consult about her ambition; know people who can advise on the subjects to study and where to train, and give access to internships or other work experience that will help her on her way.

For Appadurai, increasing this 'navigational' capacity to aspire is a vital part of empowerment, so that poorer people do not just aim higher, but increase their ability to produce a more detailed and accurate 'map' of the resources and pathways that will help them on their way. Critically, the capacity to aspire is not about individuals, but about groups of people working together to achieve change, and in the process challenging some of those cultural practices that help to keep them poor.

Working on wellbeing: core principles

Reflecting on the politics can seem quite daunting. As the book comes to a close, therefore, it is important to consider the lessons learned about the strengths of a wellbeing or quality of life assessment, and the potential it has for transformatory practice.

Many decades of local and global development initiatives have taught us that any concept, however radical and emancipatory, can be co-opted and used to advance the established agendas. This is the experience with gender, with participation, with empowerment, with rights. What ultimately matters is not the *words* but the *practice*, not the *label* but the *political commitments* that animate how it is interpreted and applied.

This is very much the case with wellbeing. Its widespread appeal is its strength – talk of wellbeing is likely to get you through the door. But the breadth of wellbeing does not necessarily tell you what to say when you get in there. The following are therefore some core principles that we recommend you adopt in taking forward work on wellbeing and quality of life.

- The power of looking at wellbeing or quality of life comes from its potential to put people and their lives at the centre of development practice and policy making. Work on wellbeing and quality of life should therefore involve a **participatory** process, which enables people to express and debate their views and reflect on any outcomes that are generated.

- A further strength of wellbeing and quality of life approaches is their ability to draw attention to **local values** and the **meanings** people make of their lives. While numbers may capture some of this, it comes through most strongly in the stories people tell and the way in which they describe what matters to them. Work on wellbeing and quality of life should therefore always involve qualitative data to complement and help interpret any quantitative scores.

- **Politics** is important to wellbeing! To be ultimately effective, psychosocial work with individuals and communities needs to be complemented by lobbying and action against regressive structures and institutions that undermine wellbeing.

- Perhaps the core contribution of wellbeing is the light that it throws on **connections** and implications across traditional boundaries of thought, sector, or academic discipline, revealing global and local as a dynamic, fluid system. Transformative practice will be achieved when the psychosocial emphasis of wellbeing and quality of life is complemented by a commitment to social and economic justice and environmental protection and promotion.

Endnotes

1. The questions were: 'Overall, how satisfied are you with your life nowadays?', 'Overall, to what extent do you feel the things you do in your life are worthwhile?', 'Overall, how happy did you feel yesterday?', 'Overall, how anxious did you feel yesterday?'

2. This is based on a calculation of the demand on earth's carrying capacity of a given lifestyle.

3. The OECD describes their domains as: '*material living conditions* (housing, income, jobs) and *quality of life* (community, education, environment, governance, health, life satisfaction, safety and work–life balance)'. <www.oecdbetterlifeindex.org/about/better-life-initiative/#question7> [accessed 24 June 2014].

4. The sub-indices are: economy, entrepreneurship and opportunity, governance, education, health, safety and security, personal freedom, and social capital.

5. These are classified as: basic human needs (nutrition and basic health, air, water and sanitation, shelter, personal safety), foundations of wellbeing (access to basic knowledge, access to information and communications, health, ecosystem sustainability), and opportunity (personal rights, access to higher education, freedom and choice, equity and inclusion).

6. Access to Gallup World Poll data is by subscription, costing several thousand pounds per year.

7. United Nations' resolution 65/309 of 25 August 2011: 'Happiness: towards a holistic approach to development.' The resolution was adopted without a vote.
8. This paragraph draws heavily on Radcliffe (2011).

References

Appadurai, A. (2004) 'The capacity to aspire: culture and the terms of recognition', in V. Rao and M. Walton (eds), *Culture and Public Action*, pp. 59–84, Redwood City, CA: Stanford University Press.

Confino, J. (2013) 'Michael Porter unveils new health and happiness index', *Guardian Professional*, 11 April <www.theguardian.com/sustainable-business/michael-porter-health-happiness-index> [accessed 24 June 2014].

Freire, P. (1972) *Cultural Action for Freedom*, Harmondsworth: Penguin.

Held, B. (2002) 'The tyranny of the positive attitude in America: observation and speculation', *Journal of Clinical Psychology* 58 (9): 965–92.

Helliwell, J., Layard, R. and Sacks, J. (2012) *World Happiness Report,* New York, NY: The Earth Institute, Columbia University. <www.earth.columbia.edu/sitefiles/file/Sachs%20Writing/2012/World%20Happiness%20Report.pdf> [accessed 24 June 2014].

Krogmeier, M., Mendes, E. and Morales, L. (2012) 'Two powerful metrics for world leaders', Gallup <www.gallup.com/poll/159155/infographic-two-powerful-metrics-world-leaders.aspx> [accessed 24 June 2014].

NDP Steering Committee and Secretariat (2013) *Happiness: Towards a New Development Paradigm. Report of the Kingdom of Bhutan,* Thimphu, Bhutan: New Development Paradigm (NDP). <www.newdevelopmentparadigm.bt/wp-content/uploads/2013/12/NDP_Report_Bhutan_2013.pdf> [accessed 24 June 2014].

NEF (2014) Happy Planet Index. Available at: www.happyplanetindex.org/about/ [accessed 16 August 2014].

OECD (2013) *OECD Guidelines on Measuring Subjective Well-being*, Paris: OECD Publishing.

Radcliffe, S.A. (2011) 'Development for a postneoliberal era? Sumak kawsay, living well and the limits to decolonisation in Ecuador', *Geoforum* 43 (2012): 240–9.

Robison, J. (2012) 'What world leaders must know now', *Gallup Business Journal*, 11 December.

Sarah C. White is a sociologist of international development and wellbeing, working at the University of Bath. She has been researching wellbeing in developing countries since 2002, with a particular focus on South Asia. She directed the Wellbeing and Poverty Pathways project in India and Zambia (2010–14). She received her PhD from the University of Bath.

Acknowledgements

This work is supported by the Economic and Social Research Council/Department for International Development Joint Scheme for Research on International Development (Poverty Alleviation) grant number RES-167-25-0507 ES/H033769/1.

Further resources on wellbeing and quality of life

Online resources

Wellbeing is a fast-developing area, and new resources are becoming available all the time. Recognizing this, there are a number of initiatives offering depositories and centres for the sharing of resources.

- Probably the biggest is the OECD's site: <www.wikiprogress.org/> [accessed 24 June 2014].
- It is also worth looking at the New Economics Foundation (NEF): <www. neweconomics.org/programmes/well-being> [accessed 24 June 2014].
- The Office for National Statistics' Wellbeing website is also useful: <www. ons.gov.uk/well-being/index.html> [accessed 24 June 2014].
- And there's also the Australian Centre on Quality of Life: <www.deakin. edu.au/research/acqol/index.php> [accessed 24 June 2014].

Books and articles

General introductions to wellbeing in international development

Copestake, J. (2008) 'Wellbeing and international development: what's new?', *Journal of International Development* 29 (4): 577–97.
Gough, I.R. and McGregor, J.A. (eds) (2007) *Wellbeing in Developing Countries: New Approaches and Research Strategies*, Cambridge: Cambridge University Press.
White, S.C. (2010) 'Analysing wellbeing: a framework for development policy and practice', *Development in Practice* 20 (2): 158–72.

Associated approaches in international development

Alkire, S. (2002) 'Dimensions of human development', *World Development* 30 (2): 181–205.
Chambers, R. (1997) 'Responsible wellbeing: a personal agenda for development', *World Development* 25 (11): 1743–54.
Hussein, K. (2002) *Livelihoods Approaches Compared: A Multi-agency Review of Current Practice*, London: Department for International Development. <www.eldis.org/vfile/upload/1/document/0812/LAC.pdf> [accessed 26 June 2014].

http://dx.doi.org/10.3362/9781780448411.013

Rowlands, J. (1995) 'Empowerment examined', *Development in Practice* 5 (2): 101–7.
Rowlands, J. (1997) *Questioning Empowerment: Working with Women in Honduras*, Oxford: Oxfam.
Sen, A. (1993) 'Capability and well-being', in M. Nussbaum and A. Sen (eds), *The Quality of Life*, pp. 30–53, Oxford: Clarendon Press.

Subjective wellbeing

Diener, E. (2000) 'The science of happiness and a proposal for a national index', *American Psychologist* 55 (1): 34–43.
OECD (2013) *OECD Guidelines on Measuring Subjective Well-being*, Paris: OECD Publishing.

Psychological wellbeing

Deci, E.L. and Ryan, R.M. (2008) 'Hedonia, eudaimonia, and well-being: an introduction', *Journal of Happiness Studies* 9 (1): 1–11.
Ryan, R.M. and Deci, E. (2001) 'On happiness and human potentials: a review of research on hedonic and eudaimonic well-being', *Annual Review of Psychology* 52: 141–66.
Ryff, C.D. (1989) 'Happiness is everything, or is it? Explorations on the meaning of psychological well-being', *Journal of Personality and Social Psychology* 57: 1069–81.

Quality of life

Hagerty, M.R., Cummins, R.A., Ferriss, A.L., Land, K., Michalos, A.C., Peterson, M., Sharpe, A., Sirgy, J. and Vogel, J. (2001) 'Quality of life indexes for national policy: review and agenda for research', *Social Indicators Research* 55 (1): 1–96.
Lau, A.L.D., Cummins, R.A. and McPherson, W. (2005) 'An investigation into the cross-cultural equivalence of the personal wellbeing index', *Social Indicators Research* 72 (3): 402–30.

Advocacy of happiness and wellbeing measures in national and international policy

Helliwell, J., Layard, R. and Sacks, J. (2012) *World Happiness Report*, New York, NY: The Earth Institute, Columbia University. <www.earth.columbia.edu/sitefiles/file/Sachs%20Writing/2012/World%20Happiness%20Report.pdf> [accessed 24 June 2014].
NDP Steering Committee and Secretariat (2013) *Happiness: Towards a New Development Paradigm. Report of the Kingdom of Bhutan*, Thimphu, Bhutan: New Development Paradigm (NDP). <www.newdevelopmentparadigm.bt/wp-content/uploads/2013/12/NDP_Report_Bhutan_2013.pdf> [accessed 24 June 2014].
OECD (2013) *OECD Guidelines on Measuring Subjective Well-being*, Paris: OECD Publishing.

Stiglitz, J.E., Sen, A. and Fitoussi, J.P. (2009) *Report of the Commission on the Measurement of Economic Performance and Social Progress*, Paris: Commission on the Measurement of Economic Performance and Social Progress. <www.stiglitz-sen-fitoussi.fr/documents/rapport_anglais.pdf> [accessed 22 June 2014].

United Nations (2011) 'Happiness: towards a holistic approach to development', Resolution 65/309, Sixty-fifth session, Agenda item 13.

White, S.C, Gaines, S.O. and Jha, S. (2012) 'Beyond subjective well-being: a critical review of the Stiglitz report approach to subjective perspectives on quality of life', *Journal of International Development* 24 (6): 763–76.

Buen vivir

Radcliffe, S.A. (2011) 'Development for a postneoliberal era? Sumak kawsay, living well and the limits to decolonisation in Ecuador', *Geoforum* 43 (2012): 240–9.

The need for caution in interpreting quantitative measures

Deaton, A. (2011) *The Financial Crisis and the Well-being of Americans*, NBER Working Paper No. 17128, Cambridge, MA: National Bureau of Economic Research (NBER). <www.nber.org/papers/w17128.pdf> [accessed 24 June 2014].

Frey, B.S. and Gallus, J. (2013) 'Subjective well-being and policy', *Topoi* 32 (2): 207–12.

Ravallion, M. (2011) *On Multidimensional Indices of Poverty*, Poverty Research Working Paper 5580, Washington, DC: World Bank. <https://openknowledge.worldbank.org/bitstream/handle/10986/3346/WPS5580.pdf?sequence=1> [accessed 24 June 2014].

Schwarz, N. (1999) 'Self-reports: how the questions shape the answers', *American Psychologist* 54 (2): 93–105.

Economics and happiness

Graham, C. (2011) 'Does more money make you happier? Why so much debate?', *Applied Research in Quality Life* 6: 219–39.

Layard, R. (2006) 'Happiness and public policy: a challenge to the profession', *Economic Journal* 116 (March): C24–C33.

Critical perspectives on wellbeing

Held, B. (2002) 'The tyranny of the positive attitude in America: observation and speculation', *Journal of Clinical Psychology* 58 (9): 965–92.

James, W. (2008) 'Well-being: in whose opinion, and who pays?', in C. Jimenez (ed.), *Culture and Well-being: Anthropological Approaches to Freedom and Political Ethics*, pp. 69–79, London: Pluto Press.

Nussbaum, M.C. (2012) 'Who is the happy warrior? Philosophy, happiness research, and public policy', *International Review of Economics* 59 (4): 335–61.

O'Neill, J. (2006) 'Citizenship, well-being and sustainability: Epicurus or Aristotle?', *Analyse & Kritik* 28: 158–72.

Sointu, E. (2005) 'The rise of an ideal: tracing changing discourses of wellbeing', *Sociological Review* 53 (2): 255–74.

Personal happiness

Burkeman, O. (2012) *The Antidote: Happiness for People Who Can't Stand Positive Thinking*, Edinburgh: Canongate.

Haidt, J. (2006) *The Happiness Hypothesis: Putting Ancient Wisdom to the Test of Modern Science*, London: William Heinemann.

Wellbeing measures, tools, and indices

Satisfaction with Life Scale

This is available at <http://internal.psychology.illinois.edu/~ediener/SWLS. html> [accessed 26 June 2014]. Anyone using the scale must give credit to its authors: Ed Diener, Robert A. Emmons, Randy J. Larsen, and Sharon Griffin. For more information, see Diener, E., Emmons, R.A., Larsen, R.J, and Griffin, S. (1985) 'The Satisfaction with Life Scale', *Journal of Personality Assessment* 49: 71–5.

The Satisfaction with Life Scale asks people to respond to five statements using a seven-point scale (where 1 = strongly disagree and 7 = strongly agree).

The statements are:
1. *In most ways my life is close to my ideal.*
2. *The conditions of my life are excellent.*
3. *I am satisfied with my life.*
4. *So far I have gotten the important things I want in life.*
5. *If I could live my life over, I would change almost nothing.*

Cantril Self-anchoring Striving Scale

The Cantril Self-anchoring Striving Scale was designed by Hadley Cantril (1965). It has become widely used since being adopted by Gallup in its World Poll of more than 150 countries, and in its daily poll of America's wellbeing (Gallup-Healthways Well-Being Index). For more information on the original version, see Cantril, H. (1965) *The Pattern of Human Concerns*, New Brunswick, NJ: Rutgers University Press. The Gallup version of this scale is available at <www.gallup.com/poll/122453/understanding-gallup-uses-cantril-scale.aspx> [accessed 24 June 2014].

The Cantril Self-anchoring Scale as used by Gallup consists of the following questions.

Please imagine a ladder with steps numbered from zero at the bottom to 10 at the top.

The top of the ladder represents the best possible life for you and the bottom of the ladder represents the worst possible life for you.

i. *On which step of the ladder would you say you personally feel you stand at this time? (ladder-present)*
ii. *On which step do you think you will stand about five years from now? (ladder-future)*

Personal Wellbeing Index

This is available at <www.deakin.edu.au/research/acqol/instruments/wellbeing-index/pwi-a-english.pdf> [accessed 24 June 2014].

The questions are answered on a 10-point scale, where zero means the person feels completely dissatisfied; 10 means he or she feels completely satisfied; and 5 is neutral (i.e. she or he feels neither satisfied nor dissatisfied). The scale comprises the questions set out below.

Part I (optional item): satisfaction with life as a whole

Thinking about your own life and personal circumstances, how satisfied are you with your life as a whole?

Part II (Personal Wellbeing Index)

How satisfied are you with:
1. *your standard of living?*
2. *your health?*
3. *what you are achieving in life?*
4. *your personal relationships?*
5. *how safe you feel?*
6. *feeling part of your community?*
7. *your secure future?*
8. *your spirituality and religion?*

The International Positive and Negative Affect Schedule Short Form (I-PANAS-SF)

For more information, see Thompson, E.R. (2007) 'Development and validation of an internationally reliable short-form of the Positive and Negative Affect Schedule (PANAS)', *Journal of Cross-Cultural Psychology* 38 (2): 227–42.

Question, measure, and item order

Question: *Thinking about yourself and how you normally feel, to what extent do you generally feel:*

Upset
Hostile

Alert
Ashamed
Inspired
Nervous
Determined
Attentive
Afraid
Active

Answer scale: never   1   2   3   4   5   always

The Warwick–Edinburgh Mental Well-Being Scale (WEMWBS)

Information on the scale is available at <www2.warwick.ac.uk/fac/med/research/platform/wemwbs> [accessed 24 June 2014].

Below are some statements about feelings and thoughts.
Please tick the box that best describes your experience of each over the last 2 weeks.

Statement	None of the time	Rarely	Some of the time	Often	All of the time
I've been feeling optimistic about the future	1	2	3	4	5
I've been feeling useful	1	2	3	4	5
I've been feeling relaxed	1	2	3	4	5
I've been feeling interested in other people	1	2	3	4	5
I've had energy to spare	1	2	3	4	5
I've been dealing with problems well	1	2	3	4	5
I've been thinking clearly	1	2	3	4	5
I've been feeling good about myself	1	2	3	4	5
I've been feeling close to other people	1	2	3	4	5
I've been feeling confident	1	2	3	4	5
I've been able to make up my own mind about things	1	2	3	4	5
I've been feeling loved	1	2	3	4	5
I've been interested in new things	1	2	3	4	5
I've been feeling cheerful	1	2	3	4	5

Inner wellbeing

For more information, see Chapter 5, or White, S.C., Gaines Jr., S.O. and Jha, S. (2013) 'Inner wellbeing: concept and validation of a new approach to subjective perceptions of wellbeing – India', *Social Indicators Research* <http://dx.doi.org/10.1007/s11205-013-0504-7>.

The table below lists the inner wellbeing questions used in rural India in 2013. With each question, five possible answers were offered, providing an ordered scale of options from strong negative through neutral to strong positive wellbeing.

Economic confidence

1.1 How well would you say you are managing economically at present?

1.2 If guests come do you feel you can look after them in the proper way?

1.3 Do you feel that people around are richer than you?

1.4 How confident do you feel that your children will have a better life than you have had?

1.5 How well could you manage if something bad were to happen (e.g. illness in the family)?

Agency and participation

2.1 If there is a village meeting do you have an opportunity to voice your opinion?

2.2 If official decisions are made that affect you badly, do you feel that you have power to change them?

2.3 Do you feel that you are heard (beyond family)?

2.4 How confident do you feel that the community can get together to take action?

2.5 How much freedom do you have to make your own decisions about the things that matter to you?

Social connections

3.1 Do you know the kind of people who can help you get things done?

3.2 When do you get to hear about gossip in the community?

3.3 How much can you trust people beyond your immediate family to be with you through bad times?

3.4 What proportion of people in the community are helpful to you?

3.5 Even when others are around, how often do you feel alone?

Close relationships

4.1 How well do you get along amongst yourselves?

4.2 If there is a problem in your family, how easily can you sort it out?

4.3 When your mind/heart is troubled/heavy, do you feel there is someone who you can go to?

4.4 How much do people in your house care for you?

4.5 How uneasy are you made by the amount of violence in your home?

(continued)

Physical and mental health

5.1 Do you ever have trouble sleeping?

5.2 Do you have the strength that you need for your daily work?

5.3 Do you suffer from tension?

5.4 How much do you worry about your health?

5.5 Do you feel that you have to do more work than you are able to?

Competence and self-worth

6.1 How well have you been able to overcome life's difficulties?

6.2 How far do you feel you are able to help other people?

6.3 To what extent do you have faith in yourself?

6.4 How close would you say you are to accomplishing what you had hoped for at this time of your life?

6.5 Looking to the future, how confident do you feel that you will be able to fulfil your responsibilities?

Values and meaning

7.1 How well are your gods and goddesses looking after you?

7.2 How lucky have you been in your life?

7.3 How much peace do you experience in your mind/heart?

7.4 To what extent would you say that you fear harm from witchcraft or evil powers?

7.5 To what extent do you feel that life has been good to you?

Index

http://dx.doi.org/10.3362/9781780448411.014